WITHDRAWN

a strategy for
public library
change:

PROPOSED PUBLIC LIBRARY
GOALS - FEASIBILITY STUDY

Allie Beth Martin
Project Coordinator

Public Library Association
American Library
Association

1972

International Standard Book Number 0-8389-3106-5 (1972)

Library of Congress Catalog Card Number 72-000062

Copyright ⓒ 1972 by the American Library Association

Printed in the United States of America

Sponsored by the American Library Association

Funded jointly by the Council on Library Resources

and by the National Endowment for the Humanities

Project Advisory Committee:

Milton Byam, Department of Library Science, St. John's
University; Chairman
John Anderson, San Francisco Public Library
Julia Losinski, Prince Georges County Memorial Library,
Hyattsville, Maryland
Lowell Martin, Columbia University, School of Library Service
Charles Robinson, Baltimore County Public Library, Towson,
Maryland
Dorothy Sinclair, Case-Western Reserve School of Library Science
Eleanor Smith, Library Service Program Officer, USOE Region 2,
New York
Keith Doms, Free Library of Philadelphia; Consultant
Gerald Born, Executive Secretary, Public Library Association;
ALA Liaison
Forrest R. Carhart, Library Technology Project

Project Staff:

Allie Beth Martin, Project Coordinator
Jan Blakeley, Literature Searcher
Martha Gregory, Secretary
Becky Connelly, Typist
Casey Parkhurst, Typist

CONTENTS

Introduction

The fate of the American institutional phenomenon, the public library, is in question. Its position has never been truly secure in terms of general use or public support except in the large cities until recent years, and for a few short periods of marked progress countrywide.

The wave of Carnegie buildings shortly after the First World War made public libraries suddenly visible. Contrary to popular belief still held by some, no accompanying service support was provided by Carnegie for the institution behind these monumental facades. A spurt of widespread public library system development was stimulated by the Library Services and Construction Act in the '50's and '60's. Federal seed money encouraged state and local support. These systems made available at least a superficial library service for the greater portion of the population. Hundreds of attractive new buildings were sources of civic pride . Numerous lumbering bookmobiles plied remote byways. Albeit used by a minority, not too well understood by the masses, the public library was admired and accepted as a desirable community service.

In the late '60's, the vision of ever more and better libraries began to fade. Although the population was increasing, use began to decline in terms of book circulation. Today, financial support, never too secure, is diminishing at the same time that costs of operation continue to rise. Societal changes shaking all established institutions to their foundations also threaten to engulf the public library. Its most enthusiastic supporters are hard pressed in the face of the harsh, cold, scrutiny of rebellious taxpayers. The public library is further endangered by the emergence of new services, agencies, institutions--apparent competitors, threatening to replace it.

In broad terms these are the problems confronting public libraries today. In spite of gloomy conditions thoughtful library leaders are saying that opportunities have never been more promising. These are the people who say that libraries should call a halt on "business as usual," based on what is felt "to be good for the community." Instead, planning, research, development and service should begin with the user and his real needs. If this is done, those taking a positive approach say that a vital, purposeful agency will emerge which will replace the passive, peripheral institution which, in the past, has waited for people to seek its service. Community services which the public library can best perform are needed and will be increasingly necessary in light of societal developments anticipated for the remainder of this century. Public libraries need not be doomed to extinction. They are on the threshold of renascence. How must they function if they fulfill this new promise? What _is_ the state of the public library today and what _should_ it be in the last quarter of this century?

How can these questions be answered? Through another study of the scope of the _Public Library Inquiry_, which did indeed have an influence on public development in the '50's? Through research and experimentation? Are the answers already available but unknown or unused by library practitioners?

The need for answers to these questions resulted in this Feasibility Study of the Proposed Public Libraries Goals Project, sponsored by the Public Library Division of the American Library Association under a grant from the Council on Library Resources and the National Endowment for the Humanities. This is the report of the feasibility phase prepared for the Executive Board of the Public Library Association.

Method of Study

Public library leaders had expressed the need for a study which would provide direction for public libraries since 1968 when Helen Fry, president of the Public Library Association, appointed a Public Library Study Committee. The committee prepared a proposal for a feasibility study and the Public Library Association was granted $24,192 for the accomplishment of this task in January 1971 by the Council on Library Resources and the National Endowment for the Humanities.

A project advisory committee was appointed, a project coordinator was selected and work proceeded under the direction of the committee as follows:

A. The Advisory Committee identified a series of problems which face public libraries and cannot be met with present resources of manpower and finance or by traditional methods. Examples of the most pressing are:

1. To develop new patterns of service to meet the needs of the disadvantaged, the handicapped, and the institutionalized, minorities and the aging.
2. To redress the imbalance between the financial resources of the central cities of metropolitan complexes, which have in the past developed and serviced major reference and research collections, and those of the suburbs whose residents now make the greatest use of the collections but contribute little to their support.
3. To reorganize public library service, recognizing that traditional organization by local governmental units is evidently inadequate, due to increasing costs of service, the growing quantity and complexity of

information demanded, and the mobility of users of libraries.

4. To utilize computer techniques and hardware to provide information to users, and to simplify and speed up routine processes within libraries.
5. To find new ways to serve sparsely populated areas, in view of the continuing decline in rural population.
6. To relate and coordinate public libraries with other types of libraries serving much the same clientele.

B. Following appointment of the Project Coordinator, Allie Beth Martin, the Advisory Committee met in June, 1971 and completed plans for implementation and a timetable for completion.

C. Work of the project began with a literature search which identified items pertinent to the points for study as outlined in the project proposal. This provided a record of public library development since the <u>Public Library Inquiry</u>. In addition, a search was made for related research in progress and as many as possible of the investigators were interviewed personally or contacted by mail.

D. A series of interviews and questionnaires were directed to 306 libraries and individuals with a 69 percent response. (See Table I)

1. Personal interviews of 63 library leaders in various sections of the country were conducted. Interviewees were asked to respond to open-ended questions concerning the state of the public library, its major problems, its goals and the need for a major study or investigation.
2. A questionnaire seeking the same information was addressed to a sample of 92 libraries which were identified as "exemplary." Both this sample and the interview group included libraries of varying sizes and respondents varied in age from recent entries into the profession to those nearing retirement.
3. A similar questionnaire was addressed to all state libraries, all Regional Program Officers of the Bureau of Libraries and Educational Technology and all ALA accredited library schools. Information regarding studies, surveys, research in progress relating to the project was solicited from these. Responses from library schools included two groups of library school students.
4. A questionnaire was addressed to the 60 libraries in the original <u>Public Library Inquiry</u> sample to determine

TABLE I

Questionnaires and Interview Contacts	Distributed	Returns	Percent of Return
1. Libraries in the Public Library Inquiry Sample	60	54	89%
2. State Library Agencies	50	39	78%
3. Regional Program Officers Bureau of Libraries and Educational Technology	9	6	67%
4. ALA Accredited Library Schools	55	32	58%
5. Exemplary Libraries	92*	62	67%
6. Non-Librarians	40	20	50%
	306	212	69%

*Includes 15 from the Public Library Inquiry sample.

        in general terms their status today and their present policies regarding the recommendations of the Public Library Inquiry.

5. Questionnaires were directed to a selected group of 40 non-librarians seeking their views of the public library today in broad terms and of the societal factors affecting it.

E. A second meeting of the Advisory Committee was held in September, 1971 to receive a progress report and plan concluding stages of the feasibility study.

F. The first draft of the report was sent to the Advisory Committee in December, 1971. Committee recommendations were incorporated and a second draft sent to the committee and to the Public Library Executive Board prior to ALA Midwinter, Chicago, January, 1972. Further recommendations were incorporated in this the final report. This report synthesizes these findings as follows:

1. Studies the societal factors affecting the public library.
2. Examines the development of the public library in the 20-year span since the Public Library Inquiry (1950-70).
3. Reports its current status in terms of major strengths and weaknesses.
4. Makes recommendations for the next phase of the Public Library Goals Study.

    For this study, "goals" are interpreted as what the public
library hopes to achieve or attain and synonymous with: intent,
purpose, objective and aim.

1. Societal Forces

What are the demographers, the urban scientists, the sociologists, the economists saying that will help foretell the future of libraries?

Change

The major force is change itself, constantly accelerating. If this is true, why attempt to anticipate the future?

> There are many good reasons for trying to imagine what the world may be like over the next thirty-three years. The most important, of course, is to try to predict conditions in reasonable detail and to evaluate how outcomes depend on current policy choices. If only this were feasible, we could expect with reasonable reliability to change the future through appropriate policy changes today. Unfortunately, the uncertainties in any study looking more than five or ten years ahead are usually so great that the simple chain of prediction, policy change, and new prediction is very tenuous indeed.[1]

We must, therefore, build the greatest possible flexibility into both library systems and programs and plan now for accommodation to continuous change.

Population Growth and Shifting Patterns

The major societal influence, cited by all who survey the world as it is and as it will be, is population growth, shifting population patterns and the accompanying ecological problems. Demographic studies in 1961 accurately projected the population shifts which resulted in urban sprawl, the decline of the cities, the great increase in numbers of professional and technical workers, the decline in the number of children of elementary school age.[2] How many librarians studied these projections and planned their services in the 1960's accordingly?

The Report of the National Commission on Population Growth and the American Future is due for publication March 15, 1972. Mrs. Joan Flint, a member of the Commission, reported the following findings which seem to be emerging in an informal interview.

1

United States population growth is slowing and should be
stabilized by the year 2000. The median age will then
be 32 as compared with the present median age of 27.6.
Family sizes will have dropped to 2 to 3 children. These
families will:

1. Place more emphasis on the quality of educational
    and other advantages for the children they do
    have;
2. Be more affluent;
3. Have more leisure.

As the median age rises:

1. The youth culture will disappear;
2. The percent of people 60 years and older will in-
    crease decidely;
3. Greater emphasis will be placed on continuing edu-
    cation through adult years.

Rural to urban population shifts will continue. The
trend will be to decentralization in growth centers,
communities of viable size. Megalopolis will continue
to develop and the inner cities will continue to be
the biggest problem.
    One quarter of the annual growth in U. S. popula-
tion comes from immigration. Since 1968, with new immigration laws, this growth has been predominantly from Asia
and Southern Europe "and may be expected to continue."[3]

    Population trends for 1970 with their implications for li-
braries have been projected by Ralph W. Conant:

Population Trends. The population of the United States
may reach 300 million by the year 2000, when, according
to some experts, it is likely to reach a plateau of
growth. While many demographers are still predicting
a doubling of population every 35 years beyond the turn
of the century, present trends belie this pessimistic
outlook. Whereas birth rates climbed steadily from
1935 to 1957, they have been receding ever since. From
an all-time high of 26 live births per thousand in 1957,
the rate had fallen below 17 per thousand by 1969--the
lowest ever recorded. The availability and widening
acceptance of new types of contraceptives plus extensive private and public efforts to promote education
and research in population control are paying off.
This gradual leveling will be noticeable by 1985.

Population statistics for the United States as a
whole are of limited value to librarians whose institutions are located in areas where population trends
are out of line with national averages. Birth rates
among blacks in central city ghettos are much higher
than among whites in other areas. Migration patterns
within and between cities are locally unique and fluc-
tuate over time. The migration patterns of cities, of
course, have a much greater impact on individual library
markets than simple population growth. It is apparent,
for example, that northern and western cities whose nonwhite populations were still below thirty percent in
1970 will experience massive shifts within the next two
decades of the character experienced by cities whose
nonwhite populations were over forty percent in 1970.
As the blacks and browns move into cities whites dis-
perse. It was evident by 1960 and even more so by 1970
that central city populations were thinning out and dis-
persing to suburbs. Thus, central cities especially in
the north and west cannot yet foresee the time when
their fluctuating populations will stabilize.[4]

A recent report for 1970 based on the latest U. S. census
releases summarized by the New York Times tells us that the nation's
poor increased 1.2 million last year; that 90 percent of these are in
metropolitan areas. Thirty percent of the total of the poor now live
in central cities. At the same time the number of poor in the suburbs
rose to 21 percent of the total. On a more heartening note the Times
noted that the number of poor people has decreased 35 percent since
1959.[5] These trends:--the continued critical conditions in the cities,
the movement of the less affluent to the suburbs, the eventual decrease
in the poverty segment--all these will influence libraries.

Discussing the present plight of the cities, Edward C.
Banfield projects: "It is impossible to avoid the conclusion that the
serious problems of the cities will continue to exist in something
like their present form for another twenty years at least."[6] His comparisons of the size of social classes, white and Negro in 1958 and
1968, show upward movement of both groups.[7] His study also shows a
movement of the urban poor to the suburbs. Banfield and others report that the problems of the cities will finally resolve themselves.

Scientific Research and Development

Taking a longer view, Arthur C. Clarke prophesies the dis-
persal of population from the cities in the 21st century.[8] He fore-
sees the impact of communications technology which he says will eliminate the necessity for people to move regularly into the cities.
Technology has been classed as second only to population as a change
agent in the years since the Second World War. Its impact will be

4

even greater in the years ahead.[9]

> At least as far as the post-industrial world in the last
> third of the Twentieth Century is concerned . . . the
> next thirty-three years may well be known as the age of
> electronics, computers, automation, cybernation, data
> processing, or some related idea.[10]

This age will require more, better educated people, and will call for
continuing re-education.

Education

Marked changes in education at all levels reflect the impact of social and technical change. Currently major emphasis is
placed on: early childhood education, individualized instruction,
equal access, optional forms of schooling.

At the college level the Carnegie Corporation has called
for the establishment of more comprehensive, largely undergraduate
colleges saying there is no need whatsoever for more research type
institutions granting the Ph.D. One hundred seventy five to 235 new
community colleges are also needed. College enrollment is expected
to continue to increase until the mid-1980's, when a decline is predicted with an increase appearing again about 1990.[11]

The greatest change in post-high school education is the
move to non-campus programs.[12] External degree programs in London
and New York (CLEP--the College Level Examination Program) and scat-
tered university programs granting credit for home study are in the
vanguard of the movement. The public library is being suggested as
a natural active component of this movement.[13] Whether these new
packaged courses eliminate the need for the library resources, or
whether some stimulation and guidance, also a place to gather, study
and exchange ideas are necessary to the new schemes, remains to be
demonstrated.

The pressure of change, of vocational dislocation, the new
leisure of the four-day week, all these and other societal influences
have resulted in an accelerated emphasis on adult education. Samuel
B. Gould, chairman of the newly appointed Commission on Non-Traditional Study, in a press release March 31, 1971, said:

> Higher education today is clearly not meeting the needs
> of a changing social structure or a vast population of
> unaffiliated students--veterans, housewives, or older
> citizens, for example. The Commission will ask how the
> individual can be served better, how institutions might
> expand present capabilities, and, in the long run, how
> the national interest may best be served . . . In broad-
> est terms, our Commission is concerned with increasing
> access to, and recognition of, post-secondary learning

by whatever means such learning is or could be achieved.[14]

The foreword to a bibliography prepared by the ERIC Clearinghouse on Adult Education stresses the growing importance of adult education:

> Since the nineteen fifties, institutions of higher learning have been experimenting with special programs to accommodate adults seeking academic degrees. In recent months, a greater interest in such programs has been sparked by several developments: The Carnegie Commission Report on Higher Education; the announcement by the New York State Regents to grant baccalaureate degrees on the basis of proficiency examinations alone; and recommendations by the American Academy of Arts and Sciences to give adults much easier access to undergraduate and advanced degrees.
>
> Besides the increasing number of adults seeking academic degrees and the financial crisis of colleges and universities, several other factors have dictated a more widespread use of special arrangements for adults to obtain degrees: travel is prohibitive for people who live at some distance away from an extension center; even for those within commuting distance, the amount of time consumed in travel is enormous; the normal time for completion of a Bachelor's degree program on a part-time basis takes about eight years; many adults find that their needs as adults are not identical with those of younger students; and the methods of instruction as well as the requirements are not really suitable for adults.[15]

Many of the items on Herman Kahn's intriguing list of "One Hundred Technical Innovations Very Likely in the Last Third of the Twentieth Century" have implications for libraries. The following selected from the list are directed to educational services, including libraries:

17. New techniques and institutions for adult education
43. New techniques and institutions for the education of children
76. Other widespread use of computers for intellectual and professional assistance (translation, teaching, literature search, medical diagnosis, traffic control, crime detection, computation, design, analysis and to some degree as intellectual collaborator generally)
86. Home education via video and computerized and programmed learning.[16]

6

The Knowledge Industry

Peter Drucker's Age of Discontinuity stresses the impact of the knowledge industry:

> By the late 1970's, the knowledge industry will account for 50 percent of the total national product. Every other dollar earned and spent will be earned by producing and distributing ideas and information and on procuring ideas and information . . . The productivity of knowledge has already become a key to productivity, competitive strength and economic strength.[17]

The Communication Industry

Developments in communications are of major importance:

1. The creation and widespread distribution of inexpensive paperbound books.
2. The great growth of news magazines and their replacement of the newspaper as the dominant printed news medium.
3. The rise of television.
4. The development of a new technology in information storage, retrieval, and dissemination.[18]

Trends in Politics and Government

Robert Salisbury's paper in The Public Library and the City, traces the history of governmental change:

1. Breakdown of political machines
2. The passing of the power of the economically and socially elite.
3. Technical experts, planners, economic, social workers preside over the operation.[19]

Stress on governmental planning at all levels is the result. Boundaries established for state planning districts and the directives of regional planning councils are dictating library system development and distribution of federal funds. Citizen participation in the new planning patterns can be anticipated. No longer can library plans be developed solely by the library administration and the board of trustees.

Reforms aimed at correcting inequalities of financial support are expected to have a major effect on the available income of the future. Recent rulings on the ad valorem tax as a base for school support may have implications for public libraries. Taxpayer resistance is forcing retrenchment in many public services including libraries.

Racial Tension

Majority-minority conflicts are expected to continue during most of the remainder of this century. Demographers project continued growth in the balance of black power in many of the major cities through the 1980's and sociologists prophesy continued tensions.[20] The climate of activism and dissent will continue to focus on the rights of other special groups, e.g. women, youth, the poor.

Leisure

Impact of the knowledge technology on the economy will contribute to new leisure patterns:

1. The shift of our economy to knowledge technology and the production of services which make it possible for people to produce more in less time, thereby facilitating reduced working hours.
2. The increased strain upon workers and thinkers of functioning in such a complex economy and society, which increases the need for leisure, escapism, and personal renewal.
3. The general availability--to educated persons at least--of easy sustenance at a relatively comfortable level, which undercuts the Horatio Alger "work" ethic.
4. The increasing growth and spread of a leisure ethic based upon changing patterns of employment and consumer behavior.[21]

"Thousands of Americans are already on a four-day week and the three-day week is emerging," according to Sylvia Porter in her syndicated column based on studies of the National Association of Manufacturers, the American Management Association and on Riva Poor's 4 Days, 40 Hours, which estimates 367 companies are already on the shorter week.[22]

Will society shaped by these changes need public libraries? Of 20 non-librarians responding to questionnaires, all felt the public library would be needed. One of these, Ferdinand Leimkuhler, head of the School of Industrial Engineering, Purdue University, emphasized: "Now more than ever emphasis is on the intellectual rather than physical aspects of human performance and the information processing aspects of production and service systems." The concluding sentence of The Year 2000 states that:

Above all, there must be a concern for perpetuating those institutions that protect freedom of human choice--not only for today's individuals and the pluralistic social

groups that would want their views represented, but more
important, for those who will follow us--those who in
the future may experience their problems differently and
would not want to find that we have already--unnecessari-
ly and unwisely--foreclosed their choices and altered
their natural and social world irretrievably.[23]

NOTES

1/ Herman Kahn, <u>The Year 2000: A Framework for Speculation on the Next Thirty-Three Years</u>. (New York, 1967), p. 1.

2/ Frank L. Schick, ed., "Future of Library Service: Demographic Aspects and Implications," <u>Library Trends</u>, v. 10, nos. 1 & 2, July-October, 1961.

3/ Informal interview January 8, 1972.

4/ Ralph W. Conant, <u>The Metropolitan Library</u> (in press).

5/ <u>New York Times</u>, November 13, 1971, p. 41.

6/ Edward C. Banfield, <u>The Unheavenly City</u> (Boston, 1968), p. 255.

7/ Ibid., p. 266-7.

8/ Television interview, December 3, 1971.

9/ Virginia H. Mathews and Dan Lacy, <u>Response to Change: American Libraries in the Seventies</u> (Indiana Library Studies, Report No. 1, 1970), p. 2.

10/ Kahn, p. 86.

11/ <u>New York Times</u>, October 7, 1971, p. 46.

12/ Ernest Boyer, "Big Move to Non-Campus Colleges," <u>Saturday Review</u>, July 17, 1971, p. 46-9, 58.

13/ Fred Cole, President, Council on Library Resources. Untitled and unpublished paper, 1971.

14/ Commission on Non-Traditional Study, 888 Seventh Avenue, New York 10019. Press Release, March 31, 1971, pp. 1-2.

15/ Stanley Grabowski,"ERIC: Special Degree Programs for Adults," <u>Adult Leadership</u>, June, 1971, p. 75.

16/ Kahn, pp. 52-5.

17/ Peter Drucker, <u>Age of Discontinuity</u> (Harper & Row, 1969), pp. 263-4.

18/ Douglas M. Knight and E. S. Nourse, eds., <u>Libraries at Large</u> (Bowker, 1969), p. 11.

10

19/ Ralph W. Conant, ed., The Public Library and the City (MIT Press, 1965), pp. 143-54.

20/ Conant, The Metropolitan Library, pp. 12-5.

21/ Kevin P. Phillips, "U. S. Predicted to Become More Leisured Society," Tulsa Tribune, October 13, 1971, B-4.

22/ Sylvia Porter, "Trend Toward Shorter Workweek Expanding," Tulsa World.

23/ Kahn, p. 413.

2. The Public Library 1950-70

Basic to the plan for the Proposed Public Library Goals Study was the decision to use the Public Library Inquiry as a "benchmark." It was the assumption that the Inquiry had been a landmark in the history of the public library and that its influence had been significant in the twenty years since its publication. What was this "benchmark," this gauge against which developments might be measured?

The project, funded by the Carnegie Foundation, encompassed nineteen studies at a cost of $250,000, a modest sum for a project of such scope by today's standards. It was carried on by a staff of researchers organized by the Social Science Research Council. The use of a team of social scientists as investigators, led by Robert D. Leigh, was unique in public library research at the time.

Dr. Leigh and his associates established the status of the public library in the late forties (the final publication of the volumes was 1950) by studying its past and its condition at the time. They also examined the developing communication industry and other societal impacts. Describing the findings of the Inquiry, Dr. Leigh[1] explained the sociologist's methodology which examined the state of an institution but did not recommend future development. He did, however, make certain recommendations and it is these which are of interest as we measure the public library today against the institution twenty years ago, look at what has happened in the interim and draw conclusions for the future.

The Inquiry is still timely, still important, worth re-reading, particularly Leigh's summary volume, The Public Library in the United States,[2] and Bernard Berelson's, The Library's Public.[3] In retrospect even a surface study of the important developments in the past twenty years reveals that the projections were accurate, that some of the recommendations even excelled Dr. Leigh's prophecies. Some of the conclusions were disputed at the time of publication but were later proven to be true.

The major recommendation of the Inquiry was the strong endorsement of the development of systems, pooling resources for strength. The Inquiry also made an earnest plea for more adequate funds for public libraries. It recommended an increase of financial support by 50 percent in the ten years following publication of the report. In fact, the median income for the Inquiry sample had increased 372 percent by 1971. The overall economy grew 242 percent in the same period.

If better library service through systems and more adequate finance can be said to be the major goals, the Inquiry truly foretold the future and had an impact upon it.

One component of the _Inquiry_, the Berelson study, drew the greatest number of dissenters and is still debated and questioned. It concluded that, contrary to the "service to all" concept traditionally held by public librarians, in truth a small portion of the population used the library; the better educated middle class. Berelson said that public libraries should not attempt to serve "all" and should concentrate on the group which it served well. He stressed the impact which the library could have if it directed its efforts toward the opinion molders of the community.[4]

The summary of the public library objectives developed by the _Inquiry_ follows.

A. General Definition of Objectives

1. To assemble, preserve, and administer books and related educational materials in organized collections, in order to promote, through guidance and stimulation, an enlightened citizenship and enriched lives.

2. To serve the community as a general center of reliable information.

3. To provide opportunity and encouragement for children, young people, men, and women to educate themselves continuously.

B. Fields of Knowledge and Interest to Which the Public Library Should Devote Its Resources

1. Public affairs; citizenship
   a) To awaken interest, stimulate reading and discussion on crucial problems;
   b) To improve people's ability to participate usefully in activities in which they are involved as citizens of their communities, the United States, and the world;
   c) To help people develop a constructively critical attitude toward all public issues and to remove ignorance regarding them;
   d) To promote democratic attitudes and values; i.e., sensitivity toward peoples by backgrounds, by knowledge concerning them and by appreciation of the dignity of the individual person; preservation of the precious heritage of freedom of expression; and understanding of the democratic processes of life.

2. Vocations
   To equip persons and to keep them equipped, for
   efficient activities in useful occupations and
   practical affairs (including vocational information, parent and home education, child care, nu-
   trition, physical health, emotional stability and
   growth, budgeting and consumer information, specialized business and industrial information).

3. Aesthetic appreciation
   To seek to give people an opportunity to improve
   their capacity for appreciation and production in
   cultural fields.

4. Recreation
   To help people make such use of leisure time as will
   promote personal happiness and social well-being.

5. Information
   To help people keep abreast of progress in the sci-
   ences and other fields of knowledge, and to furnish
   them with the detailed information required for
   their personal projects and everyday needs.

6. Research
   To serve those who are aiding in the advancement
   of knowledge.

C. Library Means for Attaining the Library Objectives

   1. Kinds of materials
      Library collections are founded on the printed page,
      but should be supplemented by films, recordings, and
      radio; also by lectures, forums, and discussion groups.

   2. Availability of materials
      By selection and organization libraries should make
      an educational instrument out of a welter of records;
      by cooperative acquisition, interlibrary loans, and
      book pools they should insure to their patrons ac-
      cessibility to the world's useful knowledge; their
      materials should be free to all residents on equal
      terms; and library service should be established
      where it is not available.

   3. Guidance
      Librarians should mediate between seekers for know-
      ledge and the recorded materials which contain and
      increase knowledge, thus eliminating the gap between
      the seekers and the sources of information and ideas.

4. Stimulation and leadership
   Libraries should have a positive program of stimulation in the use of library materials, selecting
   subjects for emphasis with the view to replacing
   indifference by interest, and of exercising an influence on what people think about, without attempting to tell them what conclusions they should reach.

   The library, in cooperation with all other agencies
   of education and information, should seek to increase the competence of people to form sound judgments and to realize that they should not only
   understand about important public problems, but
   also express their opinions and act in accordance
   with their judgment. The library should assist in
   the establishment and improvement of community group
   programs, and adapt programs to the interests of
   special groups. At the same time, the library's
   duty remains that of providing reliable information
   on all sides of controversial questions.

5. Emphasis
   During the next four years (1948-52), librarians
   should change the intensity, the duration, and even
   the nature of their services so that they will contribute directly to the solution of the crucial problems of our time.

   They should make sure that opinion leaders and other
   citizens have the widest possible range of reliable
   information on which to base their judgments and
   action.

   Libraries should provide themselves with generous
   supplies of these materials even if by so doing it
   means some curtailment of acquisition of popular and
   general materials.[5]

Sixty libraries in 22 states comprised the sample for the
Public Library Inquiry. It consisted of a scientifically selected
random list of libraries from throughout the United States, aug-
mented by a few major libraries thought to be representative of the
best at that time.

In order to draw some comparisons and assess the degree of
acceptance of the _Inquiry_ recommendations, a questionnaire was directed to the same libraries. Fifty-four of the libraries responded
and provided information comparing their status in 1948-49, and in
1970-71. They also reacted to the major recommendations of the
Public Library Inquiry in terms of their present goals and practices.

Responses varied from "The institution is almost unrecognizable from 22 years ago!" to "Not much actual change." Two librarians indicated that they answered the original Inquiry questionnaires and were pleased to have an opportunity to report again before they retired. Seven could not find earlier library records for comparison.

Summary of Responses From the Public Library Inquiry Sample:

A. Major developments since 1948-49

The following list is significant in light of the Inquiry's original recommendations. It reflects the Inquiry's strong recommendations for systems, for larger units of service capable of performing more effectively. It is interesting that physical improvements: new buildings, branches and bookmobiles were uppermost in the minds of the respondents. A few items listed are in direct conflict with the recommendations of the Inquiry, notably the emphasis on outreach services to the unserved and least likely users, according to Berelson.

Two libraries submitted lengthy lists of new programs and services which would excite even the most cynical critic of the public library.

The respondents were free to list whatever seemed important to them. Many of the items listed below would doubtless have been indicated by others had a list of developments been presented from which choices were to be made.

	No. of Libraries Answering
New or expanded buildings	33
Addition of new media	17
Expanded service areas-- development of cooperative systems	14
New and enlarged branches	14
Outreach services to inner city, low income, minorities	14
More money--federal, state, local	13
Bookmobiles	10
New services to institutions, the handicapped	7
Larger collections	6
Improved children's services	6
Improved adult services	5
New charging systems	5
Improved management	5
New subject departments	5
Enlarged and improved staffs	5
Processing centers	4
Interlibrary cooperation	4
Withdrawing school services	3
Planning and surveys	3

16

B. Change in Income, Size of Collections and Circulation
Since 1948-49
     Another major recommendation of the _Inquiry_ was for
increased funds including federal grants. By 1970-71, the
median income for these libraries had increased 500 percent,
during a period in which the economy grew 242 percent. Leigh
had recommended an increase in library revenue by 1959 of
50 percent. Two other gross comparisons were made:

     1. Size of collections--90 percent increase (median)
         (Book costs multiplied 190 percent during this
         period.)
     2. Circulation--60 percent increase (median)

     These crude comparisons need extensive refinement
and additional data should be collected to draw precise
conclusions.

C. Relative Use by Adults and Children
     Supporting the _Inquiry's_ recommendation that public
library emphasis should be directed toward adults, 25 of the
Inquiry sample libraries reported an increase in use by
adults over children since 1947-48. Only eight reported an
increase in the percentage of use by children and four indicated no change.

D. Focus on Service to Known Users--Not Service to All
     Only one of the respondents supported this recommen-
dation of the _Inquiry_. Comments included: "Never supported
this recommendation"; "Absolutely not!"; "I thought then and
I still do feel that this reflects an attitude of intellectual
snobbery better suited to an academic institution rather than
an institution supported by all the taxpayers." Several
respondents said they did make a conscious attempt to serve
the opinion molders, as recommended by Berelson, but only as
a portion of the total service. Many cited outreach programs
designed to serve previously unserved segments of the population. In summary, the libraries say today that the measure
of library success can best be judged by the breadth of the
community reached. Over and over, "service to all" was re-
iterated as a prime objective.

E. Acquisition of Quality Materials Versus Popular Demand
Items
     It was also pointed out that "quality" might also be
"popular" and the two are not necessarily opposed. Ambi-
valence marked many of the reactions to this recommendation
from the _Inquiry_. More than one-third hedged by reporting
that they concentrated on quality but also included popular
materials if of "acceptable quality." Another third said

they tried for a balance of popular and quality materials.
Three respondents stated flatly that they bought what people
wanted and in the same vein, one said, "Librarians have
failed to demonstrate that their standards are so superior
that they should be imposed on others. Censorship is rampant
in the guise of selecting quality."

In many of these libraries, popular demand is met with
rental services and paperbacks. The central library in the
system concentrates on quality resource materials, the
branches stock a greater proportion of popular demand items.

F. Informational and Educational Materials Stressed Over
    Recreational Material

Respondents were almost evenly divided in support
and denial of this recommendation from the Inquiry. Those
who said they stressed informational and educational materials
indicated they left recreation to the Recreation Department.
Those who said they included a balance of information, educational and recreational materials pointed out that increased leisure time of many people, outreach programs and
response to what people want made inclusion of recreational
materials essential. One librarian candidly admitted stressing selection of informational materials at the same time
that recreational programs were being planned to attract
more people to the library! Another quoted from the library goals statement of his library: "Educational and
informational materials shall take precedence over recreational materials." He then added wryly, "The A. D.
Little survey of this same library found a high rate of recreational use." "We try to focus on the individual and his
needs, not on rigid categories," was the thoughtful response
from another library.

G. The Library is the People's University, or The Library
    of the People's University

In the first case, the library performs an active
educational function; in the second, the library assumes a
supportive role in relation to other active institutions.
In either case focus is on out-of-school adults.
The Inquiry sample libraries reported as follows:

Library is an active agent of adult education 13
Library supports other institutions of adult
   education   19
Library does neither   5
Library does both   3

Again, answers wereequivocal. "We try." "We perform in a modest way." "It is hard to get adult education
leaders to include the library." One statement was, "The

community college is the people's university." One frank
librarian said, "We believe but we don't do."

Conclusion

Based on the same sample studied by Dr. Leigh and his col-
leagues, a good deal of what was recommended regarding the development of systems and more money for libraries became reality. The
libraries in the sample were not greatly influenced by the goals for
service which were recommended. They almost unanimously still sub-
scribe to "service to all"[6] as an article of faith. Reactions to
other major recommendations of the Inquiry are less unanimous, more
indecisive.

NOTES

       1/ Robert D. Leigh, The Public Library in the United States; The General Report of the Public Library Inquiry. (Columbia University Press, 1950) p. 241.

       2/ Ibid.

       3/ Bernard Berelson, The Library's Public (Columbia University Press, 1949).

       4/ Ibid.

       5/ Leigh, pp. 16-19.

       6/ The phrase is ambiguous. It may mean "all segments" of the community. In other contexts: library budgets, staff patterns, buildings and collections are based on the total population.

3. The Public Library Today

In response to the question, "What is the unique role of the public library?", librarians emphasized a few basic functions:

1. Free service to all without question of user purpose. It was stressed that the library's service is to <u>individuals</u> exercising free choice.
2. Provision of the widest possible range of resources for information and for decision making.
3. Serve as a repository of man's recorded past.
4. Provision of resources for educational purposes.

Also frequently mentioned were: recreational and group services, motivating and interpreting use of materials, service to adults. State librarians stressed service to all but the "student in school" and service in response to demand. Library schools spoke of the "neutral ground" of the public library and its responsibility for coordination among all types of libraries and "filling the gaps." One non-librarian said, "The public librarian is close to 'Everyman'."

<u>Libraries at Large</u> lists five "emerging library responsibilities" of libraries today. These are directed to libraries of all types but they are consistent with the functions suggested previously for the public libraries. They are more selective, and focus on priorities:

1. To support formal education, from pre-kindergarten through graduate and professional schools.
2. To sustain the increasingly complex operations of the government and the economy of the country.
3. To provide opportunities for continuing self-education and retraining.
4. To play a role in the reintegration into the society of groups now largely isolated and excluded by their lacks in education and training.
5. To provide resources for an informed public opinion and personal, cultural and intellectual growth and individuation.[1]

<u>Minimum Standards for Public Library Systems, 1966</u>, specifies two basic functions of the public library also consistent with

the responses to the questionnaires.

FUNCTIONS OF THE PUBLIC LIBRARY

The modern public library collects the printed and audio-visual materials needed to conduct the individual and group life of its constituency. It organizes and makes accessible its resources to be convenient and easy to use. It interprets and guides the use of materials to enable as many people as possible to apply in their daily lives the record of what is known. Collection; organization and distribution; interpretation and guidance--lack of any one of these results in sub-standard library service . . .

In essence, the public library provides materials and services . . .

Materials.
   Its materials are provided:
      To facilitate informal self-education of all people in the community.
      To enrich and further develop the subjects on which individuals are undertaking formal education.
      To meet the informational needs of all.
      To support the educational, civic, and cultural activities of groups and organizations.
      To encourage wholesome recreation and constructive use of leisure time.

Provision of materials means more than occasional availability. It means a supply sufficient to make the library a dependable source for most people most of the time. In addition to books, the public library selects and provides pamphlets, documents, and other non-book sources in printed form, and films, tapes, discs, and other nonprint stores of knowledge and opinion.

Services.
   The organization of material to make it easily accessible to potential users.
   Lending procedures to insure that materials may be used at the time and place desired by the public.
   Guidance to assist the user to find what he wishes, either in the material immediately at hand or in whatever library may possess it.
   A program of public information to make its resources not only available but eagerly sought by its community.

> In the last analysis, service, collections of
> books, the staff, and the physical environment re-
> commended in this statement of standards have
> meaning only as they reach all the people. It is
> to be expressly understood that each principle and
> standard noted in the following chapter applies to
> all ages and all groups in the community, and that
> a standard is not achieved if its provisions are
> met for one part of the population but not for
> another. The library which serves only the literate
> who request service is failing to meet its responsi-
> bilities just as surely as the one which provides
> too few books or makes do with ill-trained staff.[2]

Public Library Performance

What, then, is the problem if there is general agreement
about basic functions though exact terminology and priorities vary?
Statement and fulfillment are far apart. Based on the findings of
the Public Library Inquiry in 1950, lip service was being given to
these same functions when, in actuality they were not being performed.
Subsequent studies have supported the Inquiry in reporting the wide
disparity between the role stated for the public library and its
achievement.

The Gallup Poll conducted for the National Commission on
Libraries in 1967, reported only 30 percent of the adult public could
be called library users. Only 10 percent could be considered heavy
users. Thirty-five percent of these adult users said they did so to
help their children with school work. The poll further stated, "The
adult clientele can be characterized as upper middle class, rather
than a wide general public."[3]

Charles F. Bonser's Study of Adult Information Needs in
Indiana concludes: "The public library, at least as represented by
the cities selected for our study, has little relevance to the adult
population of our state. With regard to individual adult use, the
well-educated housewife is a major user, and she uses the library
primarily as a source of entertainment."[4]

Mary Lee Bundy's massive survey of use of libraries in the
Maryland-Baltimore-Washington metropolitan area states:

> The most discouraging aspect of the survey was to dis-
> cover that some twenty years after the Berelson study,
> the public library has not changed markedly in this
> respect. This period has seen major social changes to
> which we might have expected more fundamental and pro-
> nounced response on the part of public libraries. This
> is not to single out Maryland libraries in particular.
> Indeed, we believe them to be on par with and probably
> far ahead of the public library movement generally.

But the findings do suggest that public libraries
have essentially been marking time while dramatic
changes were taking place in their communities in
the U. S. generally. This is because in large
measure they are still tied to traditional commit-
ments and to traditional clienteles.[5]

A Survey of the Use of the Springfield (Oregon) Public
Library, conducted in 1971, under the direction of Perry D. Morrison
and using the Bundy techniques, reached similar conclusions. This
survey did attempt to identify likely potential users from the non-
users group.[6]

These studies have been cited because they examine patterns
of use under varied circumstances in widespread geographic regions.
Others are cited in the bibliography. While studies of library users
and non-users have not been conducted extensively, the uniformity of
their findings appears to substantiate their validity. The size and
composition of the library's active public--those who regularly con-
sume its services--have not changed much quantitatively or qualita-
tively since they were described nearly twenty years ago.[7]

If libraries are not doing what has been generally stated
should be done, what are they doing? In what ways are public libraries
performing most effectively? Answers from 100 practicing librarians
responding to the questionnaires fell in these categories:

1. The public library is serving most effectively
                                           No. of responses
   a. The middle class general reader   21
   b. Children   17
   c. Students   15
   d. Individuals who seek the educa-
      tional and cultural services of
      the library   12
2. The public library is most effective in providing
   a. Quick answer information service
      and telephone referral   19
   b. Recreational reading   14
   c. No answer   2
                                              ___
                                              100

In essence, this response says that the public library is performing
most effectively services used by a small portion of adults and by
children and young people whose numbers are declining in comparison
with the total population.

Although the quick answer or general reference service was
cited as one of the most effective services currently being performed,
it, too, has come under question. Crowley's study of the efficiency
of general reference services in medium-sized libraries in Pennsylvania
reveals that a substantial number of erroneous answers are provided

unwary patrons.[8] This one study may be too limited for generalization
but it points to the need for more critical analysis of services which
we accept without question.

Quick answer information or reference service is only one
segment of the "information" service recommended as a major public
library service of the future. Information service in the new sense
goes far beyond reliance on printed information in the library's collection or even obtained on interlibrary loan from another library.
"The public library should be the educational and access point for
specialized retrieval of all kinds of information."[9] It is, in essence, a "community answers" service, locating information in whatever source and giving active counsel to the patron.

A second group of effective services was listed by a
minority of the respondents. These were reported by
libraries which have had success with new and different services.

 a. Special services for minorities
 b. Multi-media resources
 c. Programs and other group services
 d. Service to the blind
 e. Institutional services
 f. Service by mail
 g. Service to business and industry
 h. Service as a community forum
 i. Meeting rooms
 j. Model cities programs
 k. School for dropouts
 l. Orientation to the library
 m. Service to individual community agencies

Size of library and the style of administration were cited as factors
determining effective service by four respondents. Small and medium-
sized libraries were thought to be providing more effective service
than some large systems by two respondents.

Of the 71 state libraries and library schools answering
the questionnaire, 57 responded to the question on effectively performed public library services. Their answers were in terms of the
customarily stated functions of public libraries, rather than demonstrated effectiveness.

One non-librarian summarized the outsider's view of the
public library with: "The public library has established an aura of
efficiency, intelligence, relevance, of concern for patrons."

Respondents were also asked to cite examples of libraries
which they felt were exemplary either in total operation or any part
of their program. A number said they had difficulty thinking of any
exemplary libraries and about one third of the respondents did not
answer.

In the course of the interviews a number of new and successful programs and activities were discovered by accident. When questioned about why they had not been generally reported, librarians said they did not want to seem to be tooting their own horn, or describing "how I done it good."

NOTES

1/ Knight, Libraries At Large, p. 18.

2/ American Library Association. Public Library Association, Minimum Standards for Public Library Systems, 1966 (ALA, 1966), pp. 8-10.

3/ Knight, Libraries At Large, p. 78.

4/ Charles F. Bonser and J. R. Wentworth, A Study of Adult Information Needs in Indiana (Indiana Library Studies Report No. 3, 1970), p. 113.

5/ Mary Lee Bundy, Metropolitan Public Library Users (1968), pp. 114-5.

6/ Perry D. Morrison, A Survey of the Springfield (Oregon) Public Library (Spring, 1971).

7/ W. R. Monat, "The Community Library; Its Search for a Vital Purpose," ALA Bulletin, December, 1967, p. 1309.

8/ Terence Crowley, Comparison of Reference Services in Mdeium-Sized Libraries Based on Support.

9/ Ferdinand Leimkuhler. Answer to questionnaire.

4. Critical Problems

One hundred seven respondents answered with statements falling in these major categories listed in order of emphasis:

1. Problems relating to finance
2. Public relations--the library image--failure to communicate
3. Staff--inflexibility--lack of service orientation
4. The problems of society--change--urban problems
5. Management--pattern of organization--rigidity
6. Failure to formulate objectives
7. Failure to serve all publics (minorities, deprived, new audiences, suburbs)
8. Library education--continuing education
9. Book selection policies
10. Inability to measure performance
11. Technology--failure to serve libraries, failure of libraries to adapt
12. Lack of interlibrary cooperation

Failure to formulate objectives ranked sixth in this list of urgent concerns. In reality, all of these problems affect the ability of the library to fulfill its role. They also indicate areas in serious need of study and research. Little in-depth attention has been given many of these as indicated by the paucity of information uncovered on some of the problems in the literature search. In the following summary the reaction of the respondents to major current library problems is combined with background from the literature research.

Finance

The process of interviewing and distributing questionnaires for this project extended over a three-month period, July through September, 1971. Emphasis on library finance as a major problem increased during this time. Early replies focused on services and the need for more effective public relations. Later responses indicated overwhelming concern for monetary matters, especially the library's financial base. Questions were raised about the future of the ad valorem tax as a prime source of income.

Most of the reports on library finance in the journals throughout the period 1950-71 related to amounts of money being received; increases in the '50's and '60's as the impact of federal aid

26

was noted;[1] decreases in 1969 and continuing to date.

Ratios of public library support--local, state, and federal--had been recommended on a 50-30-20 basis by Lowell Martin at the St. Louis ALA Conference, 1964. In reality, in many areas a far greater proportion of the library budget has come from federal funds. The recent shifts in federal priorities are of particular concern in library systems dependent to a large extent on federal funds. Distribution of federal funds through new channels will have an impact. New sources of revenue must be sought.

Even before the current wave of interest in management by objectives and PPBS, questions were being raised as to whether public libraries could continue to perform all services without charge. Fee based research, charges for search and deliver services, higher non-resident fees, fines and library notices have been increasingly reported. At the same time, others have been experimenting with no fines on the theory that the cost of collection and poor public relations exceeded the gains. Non-resident fees have been abandoned in favor of reciprocal borrowing privileges and statewide library cards in some instances.

The seventies brought not only financial crises but more sophisticated approaches to finance as libraries followed the lead of management in business, industry and elsewhere in government, and PPBS made its appearance in library literature. The complexities of applying management by objectives to libraries have been studied by Carl Burness at Wayne State University,[2] James D. Foust and his associates,[3] and R. L. Pfister and J. W. Milliman in the Indiana Library Studies.[4] Procedures for initiating planning-programming-budgeting in the Madison (Wisconsin) Public Library have been developed and information supplied to this Goals Study by the director, Bernard Schwab.[5]

What are the prospects for better financial support for public libraries? One would have to conclude that by and large public libraries will literally be running harder just to stay in the same place. As with other public services, it may be necessary for them to re-evaluate their objectives and reassess their goals in terms of the kinds of services and the types of clientele they should serve. But even so, it does not appear that there will be significant improvements in library funding for the foreseeable future, and public libraries will have to adjust their services and programs to the reality imposed by fiscal constraints.[6]

Library-Community Relations

A major problem frequently mentioned by respondents in interview and questionnaires but almost totally ignored in the literature and in studies in progress is the lack of two-way communication

between the library and the community. The failure of library public
relations was summarized by one state librarian in the course of the
interview with an explosive "We are invisible." Too often meager,
ineffective efforts have failed to make the public aware of the services and the resources which it owns in its libraries. Opportunities for public review of library plans and services are seldom provided.[7] Literature searches reveal a decline in reports of public
relations activity since the late fifties.[8] Most of the reports which
are published describe traditional local publicity: exhibits, posters,
booklists, newspaper columns. Library-community relations in the
broad sense have been neglected. Employment of professional public
relations personnel is the exception.

Planned library orientation for adults has been cited as a
serious need seldom met. Many potential patrons have been described
as afraid or reluctant to use the library, to ask questions, unaware
of many of its services.[9] To fulfill this responsibility librarians
must have training in the techniques of informal education using multi-
media. "The knowledge of non-librarians must be used in implementing
the new techniques of public relations."[10]

Staff--Inflexibility--Lack of Service Orientation

Manpower problems have plagued public libraries throughout
the period under study. Critical shortages were felt in the sixties.
Recruitment was in high gear. Employers clamored for applicants. At
one point it was thought the shortages in all types of libraries num-
bered 100,000. Today public libraries are reporting manpower problems
of a different sort. In the interviews one librarian said, "There is
a lack of 'service orientation.'" Another: "Lack of willingness to
change, to serve the new publics we seek to reach." One university
librarian commenting on the many opportunities challenging the public
library today, the greatest in its history, he felt, remarked sadly,
"Public librarians will never change enough to meet this challenge."
A state librarian answering the question on the most serious problem
facing public libraries said flatly, "Librarians!"

What is lacking in these librarians who are actually im-
pediments to effective service? Concern about conditions, problems,
events? Concern about availability of information? Concern that the
people who need the information have it--know how to find it? Douglas
Knight, first chairman of the National Commission on Libraries, discusses what librarians ought to be as people and poses the question:
"Are you going to serve man?"[11] Most librarians have long thought
they were doing just that, "serving," "helping," but in a passive
sense, and helping those who seek them out. Now we are told, "It is
not enough to sit back and wait for demands to be pressed by the community, The activist movement epitomized by the Social Responsibilities Round Table in ALA espouses the librarian as advocate. The
librarian must be engaged in anticipating, formulating and perhaps
even creating demands."[12] Is it possible to effect the attitudinal

change from passive to active? One study of an institute on public
library service to the inner city does describe such change.[13]

The "Outreach Leadership Network," developed by Dr. Lawrence
Allen and Barbara Conroy, is an effort to prepare public librarians
in New England for leadership roles in reaching out to unserved community groups with effective programs of library service.[14] More
activist approaches are espoused by the staff of Urban Information
Interpreters, an outgrowth of the Urban Information Specialist Program
conducted at the University of Maryland in 1971.

The Problems of Society--Change--Urban--Suburban--Metropolitan

The major societal influences affecting public libraries
have already been discussed.

Most beset of all public libraries in times of crisis have
been those in the urban-suburban complex, the metropolitan libraries.
Inner cities are in tension with the surrounding suburbs, often re-
stricted like the hole in the doughnut, with declining income and
population. Resources of large central libraries are often heavily
used by a wide geographic area, perhaps the entire state. Problems
of reciprocal services develop. Large city libraries, their conditions and recommended goals, have had substantial study and survey
analysis in recent years. Their case studies have implications for
libraries of all sizes confronted with similar problems. In "Big
City Libraries: Strategy and Tactics for Change," John Frantz uses
Brooklyn as an example of a library with responsive service.[15] Lowell
Martin's Library Response to Urban Change outlines a detailed plan
for the Chicago Public Library focusing on constructive solutions
which can be applied elsewhere.[16] Development Alternatives for San
Francisco are spelled out in a massive study conducted by Arthur D.
Little, Inc.[17] Ervin Gaines addresses himself to inherent dilemmas
facing urban libraries; the necessity for centralization and strengthening research functions at the same time that the trend is to de-
centralize to reach ghetto neighborhoods.[18]

Problems of the rapidly growing suburban libraries have not
been as extensively treated. The annual program of the North Suburban Library System (Morton Grove, Illinois) provides a forum for discussing the concerns of suburban systems. In 1968, Kenneth Shaffer
directed attention to "The Suburban Library in the Affluent Ghetto,"[19]
and the following year Lowell Martin examined "The Suburban System
in Metropolitan Library Networks."[20] A fresh approach is to be found
in "The Suburban Reality and Its Implications for the Role of the
Public Library," by Gilda Nimer, one of the papers in The Library's
Public Revisited. This student paper has an aura of hope and excite-
ment and good sense missing from the observations of many older, dis-
enchanted critics. Nimer says: "The library of today, in renewing
its heritage, need not only have books available for the seeker, but
should prod its latent public, invite it, seek interplay of man with
man and not just for book alone."[21] She develops a convincing plan

for the library as a suburban cultural center. Lester Stoffel examines the "Large City Library From the Viewpoint of the Suburban Library,"[22] and discusses their relationship.

Scholars from other disciplines have examined urban library problems and offered solutions in two important institutes: 1) the 32nd Annual Conference of the University of Chicago on the Public Library in the Urban Setting, and 2) the M.I.T. Conference which resulted in the often-quoted The Public Library and the City, edited by Ralph Conant. Dr. Conant is now revising and updating this volume which is scheduled for publication in 1972, under the title, The Metropolitan Library.

Rural public library service has been largely overshadowed by urban-suburban crises in recent years.

Management--Patterns of Organization--Styles of Leadership

The literature of public library management in the contemporary sense is meager. Library administration in the '60's was influenced by Wheeler and Goldhor in Practical Administration of Public Libraries.[23] Dorothy Sinclair's practical volume, The Administration of the Small Public Library, provides a serviceable, basic statement.[24] Roberta Bowler's Local Public Library Administration, also a practical guidebook, is being updated at this time.[25]

Recognition of trouble in library management emerged in the late 1960's, with a spate of commentary in the journals. Mushrooming systems were placing unexpected demands on library directors, who were unprepared for their new and complex responsibilities by temperament or training. Ruth May Maloney's survey of average directors of large public libraries indicated no significant change in the characteristics of directors since 1930. She concludes that librarians are status quo and may stay that way.[26] Flaws in the system concept are now being voiced as libraries seek autonomy and withdraw. The suggestion has been made that the fault may not be in the systems but in the way they are run.

Edward J. Hess examined the types of human organization found in libraries and recommended that they should move from consultative to participatory management, provide training for group participation and delegate decision-making powers. Least effective management factors observed in his studies were performance goals and training.[27]

The human aspects of library management were examined by librarians and educators in the July, 1971 Library Trends, which deals with "Personnel Development and Continuing Education in Libraries."

> A major dilemma, one we can no longer afford to ignore, faces all librarians. The dilemma is: how can we optimally integrate the technical and human resources that we manage toward achieving the library's service mission and, at the same time, manage working

arrangements and role relationships so that people's needs for self-worth, growth, and development are significantly met in our libraries?[28]

One non-librarian stated succinctly, "Public libraries must first lick their management problems." The importance of using management experts from outside librarianship was stressed. The contributions of the political scientists and public administrators to library administrators to library administration are emphasized by Ernest DeProspo.[29]

The advantages of a library board as a management partner vis-a-vis direct authority from the governmental jurisdiction has been weighed. While boards have assumed a more advisory role in some areas, trustees are still an active force in public library management generally. If they are to remain abreast of the changing public library scene and fulfill an active policy-making role, trustees, also, need continuing education and revitalization. Urban trustees feel a lack of responsiveness to the critical problems of the large cities and are currently forming a new organization.

Public Library Trustees in the 1960's were described by Mildred Batchelder.[30] The basic guide for library boards is still Virginia Young's Library Trustee, a practical guidebook.[31]

Failure to Formulate Objectives

This was the sixth major problem cited by respondents. It verifies the need for the present project. Critics of public libraries emphasize the necessity for clearly defined, universal goals and deplore the vagueness and haphazard formulation of presently existing objectives.[32] Others say universal goals are not practical, or desirable, except in the broadest sense. Instead, each library must develop its own goals which are determined by the needs of the particular community.

Edward Banfield asserts that many of our library services are already obsolete and are the business of some other public or private agency. If he is right, libraries that fail to re-evaluate objectives in terms of current demands may find their support gradually dwindling relative to other services.[33]

Failure to Serve All Publics

Those who not only recite "service to all" but attempt to put the concept in practice recognize the widening gap between concept and reality. Publics, heretofore relatively unserved and unresponsive to traditional service include: the disadvantaged, ethnic minorities, the illiterate and semi-literate, residents of institutions, and the aging. To date, a great deal has been written, numerous experiments have been reported. In fact, as reported in the literature these groups have received a major investment in library time, energy, and money in the last five years. Yet, few reports and

evaluations indicate real success, or propose principles and techniques which, if generally applied, would assure success in serving
these and other unserved groups. Two summaries describing a wide
range of activities, Henry Drennan's "War on Poverty"[34] and John Frantz'
"Outreach or Oblivion,"[35] cover the breadth and variety of these
efforts. Evaluations of these services to special library audiences
suggest approaches which may be successful if tradition, institutional
lethargy and professional resistance can be overcome. Program factors
which could insure a measure of success have been advanced by Claire
Lipsman who has studied public library service to the disadvantaged.
These program factors are:

1. Staff which can communicate effectively with
   the community.
2. The library, an integral part of the community,
   involved and demonstrably understanding the
   community dynamics.
3. Freedom for staff to make autonomous decisions,
   independent of established system patterns of
   operation.
4. Materials selected to meet the needs of users
   (heavily weighted with multi-media) not necessarily conforming to traditional selection
   policies.
5. Effective publicity which will insure awareness.[36]

Library Education--Continuing Education

There was general expression from the respondents that
library education is failing to respond to the educational needs of
public libraries either in the formal academic program leading to a
degree or in meeting continuing education needs.
Criticism was expressed by the library educators themselves.
One of the most positive statements was made by a library school dean
who criticized library educators for failure to lead. Other educators
had positive recommendations: 1) revise curriculum; 2) more emphasis
on human relations, management, automation; 3) more inter-disciplinary
programs; 4) more emphasis on continuing education; 5) more opportunities for faculties to update themselves. Extensive studies of the
professional development of librarians have been conducted by James
Kortendick and Elizabeth W. Stone of Catholic University.[37]
Leaders among public librarians and state librarians expressed the feeling that much of library education de-emphasized
public libraries, treated them as inferior to academic libraries,
although notable exceptions were cited. Many felt library education
was behind the times; one said library schools are doing a good job
training for the '50's. Exchanges, internships, continuing education
for faculties as well as for practitioners were recommended. Although
a cautionary note was occasionally injected--reminders that too much

is expected of education--criticism was so general, so positive, that it should not be discounted.

Out of 83 responses regarding the effectiveness of library schools in preparing public librarians, ratings were as follows:

Good	4
Fair	31
Poor	40
Improving	8
	83

Most frequent comments were: "too isolated," "need more attention to management, more continuing education." This presupposes that public librarians will be permitted to attend if there are opportunities or that it will be possible to participate in the re-education process without leaving home. One respondent said, "If the public library is to survive it must have more support from education." Some reservation was expressed about the ability of library schools to provide the needed continuing education. It was suggested by two respondents that continuing education for public librarians should properly be the responsibility of the state library. Public librarians should help in shaping revised curricula. Two deans said they could not respond to the questionnaire as they knew very little about public libraries!

One library school class answered the questionnaire collectively. They recommended more attention to supervision, interpersonal relations, more on-the-job training and questioned whether it is possible to "teach creativity, responsibility, the "service attitude."

The contents of issues of the Journal of Education for Librarianship were checked for the past five years. The number of papers relating to the education of public librarians was negligible. Jesse Shera's frequently quoted, "What is Past is Prologue; Beyond 1984," summarizes the condition of library education with the statement that the library school curriculum is "dead" and must be changed.[38] The program must be both interdisciplinary, and specialized. The library schools cannot remain isolated institutions. The following is a partial list of subjects or areas which were thought to need more attention as a part of the degree program and in continuing education.

1. Management
    a. Establishing goals and objectives
    b. Participatory management
    c. Fiscal management
    d. PPBS
    e. Operations research
2. Human relations
3. Staff Development
4. Public relations techniques

  5. Multi-media resources
  6. Orientation--Introducing patrons to the library
  7. Group process
  8. Applications of technology
  9. Selection of new materials--revised policies
 10. Library adult education

Selection Policies

     The uncertainty, ambivalence and stress within librarian-
ship is epitomized in the numerous current problems relating to one
of the most basic of library operations--the selection of resources.
The concepts of selecting what is "best," of relying on time-worn
book selection policies, of pre-selection for all libraries in a system by coordinators or by committee, of selection from so-called
"standard" selection aids and lists--all are in question. "Book
selection which strives for 'best' should reappraise its stand to
serve everyone."39 The library has generally chosen its books on the
basis of standard sources. These lists may not contain what people
really want to read, or would choose themselves.
     Overwhelming productivity, the masses of materials threat-
ening to swamp any selection process, has caused larger libraries to
abandon efforts at selectivity and to resort to blanket orders,
Greenaway Plans, mass purchasing. Who selects? The individual branch
library? The pressure of demand? What one respondent called "selection by television"? The jobber supplying blanket orders may not
really "blanket" since best-sellers and heavy demand items do not al-
ways arrive automatically.
     Nor does "automatic" buying insure fulfillment of another
major set of responsibilities--those relating to balance in the collection, representation of all points of view, both sides of contro-
versy. "Giving people what they want" may mean selection by "pressure
groups." A wave of censorship has steadily increased in the '60's
and into the '70's, and shows no signs of subsiding. Throughout the
period libraries have maintained their dedication to intellectual
freedom and today their resistance is firmer than ever. To these
sensitive problems has been added another: the patron's right of
privacy.
     Selection problems are compounded when the practicalities
of the acquisition and cataloging process are added. Here better
management, careful planning, efficiency are demanded to speed up re-
ceipt of materials to insure availability when patrons need and want
them. An articulate plea dealing with what is and is not possible in
practical and provocative terms is voiced by Daniel Melcher.40
     Joint acquisitions agreements among libraries to avoid
costly duplication provide obvious opportunities for interlibrary cooperation. To date, reports of successful applications of the concept have been limited. In fact, it is being resisted by those who
insist that access to a varied selection of materials on the shelves

is what is essential.

Resistance to selection of less traditional types of materials seems to be a built-in complication. Publications of the proliferating underground press are outside the mainstream of traditional publishing and unknown to many librarians. Paperbacks, non-print media and equipment require new methods of handling. Departure from accustomed policies and processes and methods to select, acquire and merge them into the normal operations of the library must be developed.

Inability to Measure Performance

Librarians have long been telling themselves and each other that library benefits cannot be quantified, an assumption based on an axiom that social benefits are immeasurable. Difficult to do? Certainly. Impossible? Maybe. Other disciplines--medicine, social service, education--are faced with the same problems and some systems of measurement are emerging.

Taxpayers are demanding information about how much is being accomplished with their money. Specific measurement is essential to modern management based on performance. Difficult as it appears, some of the research efforts examining library use are beginning to suggest factors which may be measured practically. The major study currently underway which deals directly with these problems is the American Library Association-Public Libraries Project at Rutgers University.[41]

Technology

If the amount of writing on a topic in the library literature is an indication of its importance for the profession, automation of libraries topped everything else in the '60's. In sharp contrast, public librarians interviewed seldom mentioned automation either as an important development or as a major problem. Occasionally a respondent expressed the feeling that technology had been oversold. Ferguson's study of the sociology of information organizations compares librarians and information scientists:

> There appears to be a split between the two groups:
> the librarians resisting technical innovations in-
> volving computer applications, and the information
> specialists not only eagerly adopting these tech-
> niques but attempting to force them upon the rest
> of the information profession.[42]

Reports indicate almost all activity has been in academic libraries.[43] Of the more than 300 entries on automation in Library Literature in the period 1967-69, less than one dozen applied to public libraries; almost all in large public library systems, in state libraries, or in cooperatives such as processing centers. Applications reported were acquisitions, catalogs, circulation systems and serials control.

Automation is needed but is not proving itself. Libraries are not expressing their needs well enough.

> Computer programmers, analysts and salesmen have frequently stated that solutions have been found and that librarians are too conventional to adopt them . . . However, once they have been exposed to analysis and depth of library systems, computer people tend to take a more cautious view about the nature and extent of computer systems for libraries.
>
> Part of the lack of understanding about how libraries really operate stems from the fact that, until quite recently, only librarians were very much concerned about library procedures.[44]

Public libraries have also been reluctant to adopt other technological advances. Collections which are still limited to printed materials are anachronisms in a non-print world. In many public libraries non-print resources are still treated as an afterthought, a frill. Two technological resources with great promise at this time are the video-cassette and CATV with its potential for telecommunication as well as programming. Unless libraries make their interest known to these new industries and participate in the experimental stages the opportunity may be lost.

Robert Presthus' report on Technological Change and Occupational Response: A Study of Librarians, strikes a distressing note regarding the chances of libraries to catch up with the rest of the world:

> Substantial change often has to be imposed from outside a given occupation or institution, and some of the values of some of our librarians are, as we have seen, somewhat inapposite to demands now impinging upon their field. In this sense, it would be neither surprising nor unusual if the major thrust for automation and systems concepts would have to wait for a new generation of librarians, trained in schools that have fully incorporated the skills and concepts of a new librarianship into their teaching programs.
>
> Another alternative is that librarianship may by default allow the emerging "information specialist" groups to determine the conditions of participation in the changing library occupation.[45]

Lack of Interlibrary Cooperation

The need for more real cooperation was still considered a
major library problem in 1971, in spite of heavy emphasis in terms of
money and effort through the LSCA years (1957-to date). Indeed, thirty
of the respondents to the study felt libraries were further apart today
than in the past. Competition for funds was frequently mentioned as
a major deterrent. Often contributing to the apparent declining relationships are: rivalry among types of libraries; college and university libraries placing stricter regulations on use by outsiders;
unexpected pressures; e.g., newly established community colleges and
burgeoning urban universities place unforeseen demands on public
libraries.

On the plus side, LSCA has greatly assisted growth of public library systems and more recently with Title III, interlibrary
networks have begun to function. Unrelenting pressure from taxpayers
questioning duplicated efforts may be counted on to force continued
efforts to implement cooperation and even combined services. "Talk
and little action" has been a criticism but at least rapport, heretofore unknown, has been established and some blurring of distinction
has occurred.

R. H. Stenstrom's extensive annotated bibliography,
Cooperation Between Types of Libraries, 1940-1968, provides an ex-
cellent overview of this area of concern and sharp disagreement.[46]
It was apparent that most cooperation was still in the talking stage
in 1968, though some real experience was included. O. F. Nolting's
Mobilizing Total Library Resources for Effective Service, summarized
the barriers to cooperation:

     1. Psychological
     2. Lack of information and experience
     3. Traditional and historical (restraints)
     4. Physical and geographic barriers
     5. Legal and administrative (barriers)[47]

Two major conferences--1) Library Networks: Promise and
Performance, at the University of Chicago in 1968,[48] and 2) Cooperation Between Types of Libraries, at Allerton Park in 1964[49]--were concerned with the basic factors determining the success of cooperative
efforts and their future. Flint Purdy categorized existing examples
of programs and plans:

     A. Union catalogs and lists
     B. Cooperative development of resources
     C. Sharing resources in terms of use
     D. Communication
     E. Centralized processing
     F. Cooperatively sponsored planning and surveys
     G. Cooperative storage
     H. Cooperative computer centers[50]

A cautionary note that networks cannot replace collections adequate for the daily needs of the community was expressed by Dan Lacy.[51] T. L. Minder addressed the <u>Organizational Problems in Library Cooperation</u>, further stressing the four human factors essential for successful library cooperation:

1. Benefits for me
2. Benefits for you
3. Benefits for us
4. A referee to keep peace[52]

Major cooperative efforts have developed on diverse levels:

1. National
2. Regional--multi-state
3. State
4. Regional--multi-library
5. Urban--suburban
6. Local

All have been extensively described in the '60's and to date. At the outset accent was placed on the advantages of greatest possible informational accessibility[53] and on the advantages of shared technology.[54] Title III LSCA money was used to develop information networks in many states. Although emphasis in these networks has been on improved interlibrary loan services among all types of libraries, relatively large user groups--junior college, high school and university extension and correspondence students--have been excluded from many of these networks. Major problems in these networks have been excessive burdens felt by the strongest libraries in the network, inability to interface networks due to incompatible technology and conflicts of basic purpose.

Inter-state networks along regional lines have had broader purposes and offer promise of fulfilling needs which cannot be met within a single state but which are too complex or otherwise impractical at the national level.

	Rocky Mountain Bibliographic Center.
PNBC	Pacific Northwest Bibliographic Center, originally a bibliographic center but more recently has expanded its purpose.
WICHE	Western Interstate Commission for Higher Education.
NELINET	New England Library Information Network.
SLICE	Southwestern Library Interstate Cooperative Effort.

Most are too new for their permanent viability to be assessed.

Even systems comprised of libraries of one type serving a cluster of jurisdictions within a single state have encountered problems in recent years. In some cases systems have become unnecessarily authoritative and unresponsive to needs of different communities. Here and there individual libraries have withdrawn, preferring autonomy to the advantages of cooperation. Shaffer questions the assumptions on which these cooperative efforts developed but concludes that systems are still the best if not the only way if public libraries are to remain viable.

> Perhaps the goal of the library system in the coming decade should be less on technical resources and more upon the expertise that only can be joined together for purposes which they could not sustain individually but which only could be afforded by the new system.
> We need a new and different kind of library system in this country, one different from the realities which the Nelson Associates Survey of 1969 indicated were in existence. For although the problems which seem to have had the highest priority in library systems of the past decade have been those of providing greater accessibility to library materials and resources, the problem immediately facing the public library organized or not organized within a system in the seventies will be in terms of self-justification to the taxpayer on one hand and defense against demagogic attack on the other. The system is the best if not the only vehicle to provide the expertise for viable public libraries, strong both intellectually and fiscally. A markedly different set of priorities for the decade that is upon us is urgently indicated.[55]

Much less certainty has been expressed about relationships between types of libraries at the local level. Nearly every library queried in the study made some comment on school-public relationships. The recommendation of the New York State Commission on Education[56] that public schools should assume responsibility for all library service to children was met with an emotionally volatile response. Some of the reaction was based on past experience. Combined school-public libraries had not been noticeably effective in years past and in most instances experience dictated the wisdom of separation. Also, this is one area in which public libraries seem to be performing most effectively. In many instances, notably in small towns, in branches, and on bookmobiles, children make up more than 50 percent of total use. Few of the school libraries as they exist today are equipped to

provide services of the character available in many public libraries
year 'round, weekends and holidays.

The problem of duplication was not felt to be too critical
by the librarians queried who indicated some duplication is inevitable;
both public and school libraries are so far from meeting total needs
of children, there is enough for both to do; the services have different purposes; children should have some options; duplication should
be purposeful. This duplication is not as acceptable to patrons who
pay the bills. One library board member stated bluntly, "My children
use both the school library and the public library and they borrow
the same books. This doesn't make sense."

Schools are changing. Their survival, as we know them, is
also in question. If they become community centers used by children
and adults, day and night, twelve months a year, separate school-
public libraries will be difficult to defend.

A decline in the use of the public library by students has
set in in many areas. The crush of students which made this the
number one problem of the public library in the late '50's and early
'60's has abated. Studies of public library circulation figures show
the greatest decline in children's use. It is, however, apparently
still true that children and young prefer the public library over the
school library.[57]

Clearly, experimentation under contemporary conditions is
needed. The Commissioner of Education in New York projects pilot
demonstration projects to determine the effectiveness of joint school-
public libraries. Other sporadic joint efforts are being reported in
Arizona, New Jersey and Maine, and elsewhere. Philadelphia is experimenting with a new entity, a community library and learning center
separate from both school and public library. Based on extensive
study of both of the existing systems, the "Philadelphia Project," now
in its early stages, promises to provide an opportunity for analysis
under experimental conditions.[58]

College level users seem to continue to use whatever library
is convenient. To the commuting student, the nearest public library
is his library, not the library of the college or university. "Many
students and faculty of urban universities find their library services
elsewhere . . . Unfortunately, no one has yet devised any satisfactory
means to compensate these libraries for the services they render the
urban student."[59]

Prospects for public-college/university library cooperation
would appear to be good since college and university libraries have
more of the specialized research materials which the public library
cannot afford but which are needed for infrequent requests. In practice, greatest resistance to interlibrary cooperation comes from the
large academic libraries. Their stated function is to serve their
own academic community. They fear an onslaught of demand from less
serious users if the barriers are relaxed.

The movement toward the "University Without Walls" may
place a greater and different dependence on libraries--public and
college/university. Recommendations made to the new National

Commission on Non-Traditional Study suggest a far greater use of public libraries.[60] However, in England it is reported "students have less time for background reading" with the new packaged courses of the "Open University."[61]

Responsibility for leadership in coordinating library services at the local level is the logical responsibility of the public library. Each of the other types of libraries--school, college/ university, special--has its own clientele as a primary responsibility. All of these clienteles are also the responsibility of the public library for general services.

42

NOTES

1/ J. C. Frantz and N. M. Cohen, "Federal Government and Public Libraries; a Ten-Year Partnership," Illinois Libraries, v. 48, September, 1966, pp. 544-68.

2/ Carl G. Burness, Defining Library Objectives (Wayne State University, 1968).

3/ James D. Foust, General Economic and Demographic Background and Projections for Indiana Library Services (Indiana Library Studies, Report No. 5, 1970).

4/ R. L. Pfister and J. W. Milliman, Economic Aspects of Library Service in Indiana (Indiana Library Studies, Report No. 7, 1970).

5/ Bernard Schwab, Planning-Programming-Budgeting (Madison Public Library).

6/ Joseph Eisner, "Public Libraries; On the Skids?", Library Journal, V. 96, October 1, 1971, p. 3095.

7/ Edwin E. Olson, Survey of User Service Policies in Indiana Libraries and Information Centers (Indiana Library Studies, Report No. 10, 1970), p. 125.

8/ Fred Neighbors, MS Thesis, School of Library Science, University of Oklahoma, 1971.

9/ K. Molz, "State of the Art of Public Library Orientation," Maryland Libraries, v. 34, Winter, 1968, pp. 10-7.

10/ M. C. Hannigan, "Orientation of the Out-of-School Adult to the Use of Public Libraries," ALA Bulletin, v. 61, July, 1967, pp. 829-30.

11/ Douglas M. Knight, "Wisdom in Action: The Role of the Modern Library," Connecticut Libraries, v. 12, Summer, 1970, pp. 3-7.

12/ W. R. Monat, "The Community Library; Its Search for a Vital Purpose," ALA Bulletin, December, 1967, p. 1309.

13/ C. L. Kronus, Inducing Attitudinal Change Among Librarians, 1970, ERIC ED046407.

14/ Described in response to questionnaire.

15/ John C. Frantz, "Big City Libraries: Strategy and Tactics for Change," Library Journal, v. 93, May 15, 1968, pp. 1968-70.

16/ Lowell Martin, _Library Response to Urban Change; A Study of the Chicago Public Library_ (American Library Association, 1969).

17/ Arthur D. Little, Inc., _Development Alternatives for San Francisco_ (The author, 1970).

18/ Ervin J. Gaines, "Urban Library Dilemma," _Library Journal_, v. 94, November 1, 1969, pp. 3966-70.

19/ Kenneth Shaffer, _Suburban Library in the Affluent Ghetto_ (North Suburban Library System, 1969).

20/ Lowell Martin, _Suburban Systems in Metropolitan Library Networks_ (North Suburban Library System, 1970).

21/ Mary Lee Bundy, ed., _The Library's Public Revisited_ (University of Maryland, 1967), pp. 11-31.

22/ Lester Stoffel, "Large City Library From the Viewpoint of the Suburban Library," _Library Quarterly_, v. 38, January, 1968, pp. 90-100.

23/ Joseph Wheeler and Herbert Goldhor, _Practical Administration of Public Libraries_ (Harper, 1962).

24/ Dorothy Sinclair, _Administration of the Small Public Library_ (American Library Association, 1965).

25/ To be edited by Raymond Holt under the sponsorship of the ALA Library Administration Division.

26/ Ruth May Maloney, "Average Director of a Large Public Library," _Library Journal_, v. 96, February 1, 1971, pp. 443-5.

27/ Edward J. Hess, _A Study of Human Response to California Library Organization and Management Systems_ (Dissertation, University of Southern California, 1970).

28/ Elizabeth W. Stone, (Introduction to) "Personnel Development and Continuing Education in Libraries," _Library Trends_, July, 1971, p. 3.

29/ _Administration and Change; Continuing Education in Library Administration_, by Neal Harlow and others (Rutgers University Press, 1969).

30/ Mildred Batchelder, _Public Library Trustees in the 1960's_ (ALTA, ALA Publication No. 4, 1969), pp. 29-38.

31/ Virginia Young, _Library Trustee_ (American Library Association, 1964).

44

32/ Paul Wasserman, <u>Toward a Methodology for the Formulation of Objectives in Public Libraries; an Empirical Analysis</u> (Doctoral Dissertation, University of Michigan, 1960).

33/ Conant, <u>The Public Library and the City</u>, p. 178.

34/ Henry T. Drennan, ed., "War on Poverty," <u>Library Journal</u>, v. 89, September 15, 1964, pp. 3241-74.

35/ J. C. Frantz, ed., "Outreach or Oblivion," <u>Wilson Library Bulletin</u>, v. 43, May, 1969, pp. 848-903.

36/ Manuscript to be published by ALA.

37/ James J. Kortendick and Elizabeth W. Stone, <u>Job Dimensions and Educational Needs in Librarianship.</u> (ALA, 1971).

38/ Jesse Shera, "What is Past is Prologue," <u>ALA Bulletin</u>, v. 61, January, 1967, pp. 35-47.

39/ Kathleen Molz, "Public Library: The People's University?" <u>American Scholar</u>, v. 34, Winter 1964-65, pp. 95-102.

40/ Daniel Melcher and Margaret Saul, <u>Melcher on Acquisitions</u> (American Library Association, 1971).

41/ Ernest R. DeProspo, <u>Measurement of Effectiveness of Public Libraries</u> (Rutgers University).

42/ John D. Ferguson, <u>The Sociology of Information Organizations</u>. (Doctoral Dissertation, Columbia University) p. 193.

43/ L. Overmeyer, <u>Library Automation: A Critical Review</u> (U. S. Office of Education, Bureau of Research, 1969).

44/ Barbara Evans Markuson, "An Overview of Library Systems and Automation," <u>Datamation</u>, February 1970, p. 61.

45/ (Introduction to) <u>Library Trends</u>, July, 1971, p. 15 (Quoted from Robert Presthus, <u>Technological Change and Occupational Response: A Study of Librarians</u>, Final Report, Project No. 07-1084, Washington, D. C., Office of Education, Bureau of Research, 1970.)

46/ R. H. Stenstrom, <u>Cooperation Between Types of Libraries, 1940-1968; An Annotated Bibliography</u> (American Library Association, 1970).

47/ O. F. Nolting, <u>Mobilizing Total Library Resources for Effective Service</u> (American Library Association, 1969).

48/ Chicago University, <u>Library Networks: Promise and Performance</u>, 33rd annual conference, July 29-31, 1968 (University of Chicago Press, 1968).

49/ Illinois University, <u>Cooperation Between Types of Libraries</u>, Allerton Park Institute No. 15 (University of Illinois, 1969).

50/ Chicago University, p. 54.

51/ Dan Lacy and V. H. Mathews, <u>Social Change and the Library, 1945-80</u>, Final Report to the National Advisory Commission on Libraries, 1967.

52/ T. L. Minder, "Organizational Problems in Library Cooperation," <u>Library Journal</u>, v. 95, October 15, 1970, pp. 3448-50.

53/ Kenneth Shaffer, "Library Systems: Tough Times Ahead?" <u>Library Journal</u>, v. 96, July, 1971, pp. 2263-5.

54/ T. L. Minder, <u>Regional Library Center in the Mid-1970's; a Concept Paper</u> (Graduate School of Library and Information Science, University of Pittsburgh, 1968).

55/ Shaffer, "Library Systems: Tough Times Ahead?" p. 2265.

56/ New York State Education Department, <u>Report of the Commissioner of Education's Committee on Library Development</u> (New York, 1970).

57/ Philip S. Wilder, <u>Library Usage by Students and Young Adults</u> (Indiana Library Studies Report No. 4, 1970), p. 23.

58/ J. O. Benford, "The Philadelphia Project," <u>Library Journal</u>, v. 96, June 15, 1971, pp. 2041-7.

59/ E. G. Holley, <u>Urban University Libraries Organization and Administration</u> (Unpublished report to the Council on Library Resources, 1971).

60/ Fred Cole, Untitled working paper on the proposed role of the public library in non-traditional education. Presented to the Commission of Non-Traditional Studies, August, 1971.

61/ D. J. Simpson, "Books and the Open University," <u>Library Association Record</u>, September, 1971, p. 168.

5. Consensus on Goals

Responses from librarians answering, "What do you think the goals of the public library should be?", can be categorized as follows:

1. To provide service to all
   (stressed reaching unserved)
2. To provide information services
3. To provide adult and continuing education
4. To collect and disseminate all kinds of informational, educational and cultural materials, including non-print resources
5. To support education--formal and informal
6. To serve as a cultural center

Officially adopted statements of function and purpose were collected. Many were couched in broad generalities lifted from the public library standards and other such publications. Others reflect careful thinking and attention to the needs of individual communities.

The non-library specialists also stated specific goals which emphasized an active, aggressive role:

> The library should become more and more a center for self-development, tying in more closely with local schools, colleges, technical resource centers. It should become the community resource center for audio-visual materials, linked up with other information centers.
>
> Ian Wilson, General Electric Company

> The library should be the leader and facilitator of community life--the encourager and stimulator of borrowers.
>
> Cyril Houle, University of Chicago

The responses generally reflect two divergent viewpoints:

1. One outlook is characterized by a spirit of hope, a sense of the future which will require libraries, or some other similar institution, more than ever before. The proponents of this philosophy say librarians will become active agents serving the needs of society in positive, dynamic fashion. The advocates of this point of view are enthusiastic, even excited about the future. They temper

46

their optimism with the realization that marked change must
take place if the bright future projected is to be realized.

Three things will be required: (1) a concentrated
public relations effort which will insure two-way communication between libraries and the public at large;(2) extensive and coordinated research and experimentation; (3)
demonstration and the development of prototypes to insure
an informed basis for continuous change; and (4) a con-
certed and continuous educational effort to insure practitioners prepared to meet the constant challenge of change.

The optimistic outlook was voiced by some of the
librarians confronted with the most acute problems. It was
also espoused by non-library specialists who were interviewed. It is eloquently summarized by Virginia H. Mathews
and Dan Lacy in their statement on "Library Responsibilities
in the Next Decade," in Response to Change: American
Libraries in the Seventies:

> In summary, we can perhaps identify several
> principal and priority responsibilities for
> libraries in the next decade:
>
> 1. To support and sustain formal educa-
>   tion from pre-kindergarten through
>   graduate school, for which millions
>   of students, widely diversified as to
>   abilities and goals, will require access
>   to a greater range of media than ever
>   before.
> 2. To play an initiatory role, with other
>   agencies and institutions, in develop-
>   ing in people an orderly acceptance of
>   change and in helping them to adapt to
>   it.
> 3. To serve as both the motivator and sup-
>   plier of aspirations for the dispossessed
>   and disorganized.
> 4. To support the increasingly complex op-
>   erations of government, of science, and
>   of the business sector of the country.
> 5. To provide support, with and through
>   other agencies, continuing self-educa-
>   tion and training for people at all
>   levels of work.
> 6. To accept the individual as an indivi-
>   dual and to provide spiritual nourish-
>   ment, intellectual stimulation, cultural
>   enrichment, and information alternatives
>   to him at the neighborhood or community
>   level.[1]

2. The other outlook, a minority, might be called the "prophet of doom" response. "The public library is dying," or moving toward extinction and will soon be replaced by technology or by other types of libraries and information services. This has the ring of self-fulfilling prophecy. It is rejected by a majority of respondents, both librarians and non-librarians.

NOTES

1/ Mathews and Lacy, pp. 41-2.

6. Consensus on Another Public Library Inquiry

Although sixty percent of all who answered said, "yes," most of these qualified their response. Fourteen percent were uncertain about the need and sixteen percent said "no."

In fact most who answered this question, both pro and con, had comments and suggestions which actually negate another "Inquiry" type study. They said:

1. It should include all types of libraries--<u>not public libraries alone</u>.
2. It should be based on the user's needs, not on a survey of the past.
3. It should be updated continuously.
4. It should recognize that no set of goals could be universally applicable except in the broadest terms. <u>Each library must set its own goals based on its own community needs</u>.
5. It should result in immediate action. "We cannot wait for a lengthy study and publication which may take two or three years."

An attempt was made to obtain some direction from a sample of forty non-librarians: scholars, sociologists, political scientists, urban scientists, writers. Fifty percent responded and some of those who answered indicated they did not know enough or had no thoughts about public libraries. Of those non-library specialists answering all recommended against a major library inquiry as an answer to public library problems.

7. Recommendations--A Strategy for Public Library Change

There is a clear mandate for a program of action which will enable the public library to fulfill its unique role in performing needed community functions which will be increasingly important in light of continuing changes in society.

1. There is a widespread lack of recognition of existing strengths and of the potential for full development of the public library as a community asset among the public at large, even among libraries of all types, including the public library.

2. There are gaps in what is known about the public library as an institution and about its performance which require research and experimentation demonstration, development of prototypes.

3. Much of the research and experimentation which has been completed is little known or has not been applied through demonstration, development of prototypes.

4. There is an urgent need for concentration on training and retraining of the practitioners--those presently performing and those who will follow--to enable them to know how to establish goals for individual libraries, how to develop libraries which will continaully change with society and perform effectively in the community.

Therefore, a four-part plan of action is recommended to the Executive Board of the Public Library Association which should be given highest priority in the program of work for the Association. A concentrated public relations program, using all media, designed to made the public library more visible should be launched at all levels: national, regional, state and local.

First, a publication should be commissioned which will be an eloquent statement to direct widespread attention to the American public library as an active community agent capable of meeting the real needs of real people today and in the future. This should be presented in layman's language, designed to capture the attention and imagination of the public at the same time that it synthesizes the concerns of librarians and governing bodies of all types of libraries. A documentary film should accompany the publication.

Second, a program of extensive research and investigation will be required to provide needed knowledge for effective performance. Ralph Blasingame and Ralph W. Conant developed an outline of needed research in their report of the Rutgers Seminar in 1964-65, which is still valid, little of which has received attention to date. Conant has updated this list in The Metropolitan Library, soon to be published.

The following is a composite of these recommendations and of research needs indicated by the present Goals Study:

1. Users--Non-Users
   a. Characteristics
   b. Changes over a period of time
   c. Effects of use of library resources on patrons
   d. Differences in use patterns in different communities
   e. Special groups--Special problems of reaching:
      (1) The poor
      (2) Blue-collar workers
      (3) Early childhood
      (4) Senior citizens
2. Information Need and Supply
   a. What is required by special groups (subject specialists, various economic and social levels)? Where is it? Where should it be available?
   b. Where do people get information? How is the flow assisted, inhibited?
   c. What should be available without charge? With a service charge?
3. Societal and political Factors
   a. Attitudes of staff
      (1) Toward patrons?
      (2) Toward various classes of people?
      (3) Toward libraries?
      (4) Toward trustees?
   b. Attitudes of **trustees**
      (1) Toward changing responsibilities of libraries
      (2) Toward the community
      (3) Toward the staff
   c. Library budgets
      (1) As a reflection of community needs
      (2) PPBS--How to apply
   d. Political environment of the library
   e. Tradition and public image of library
   f. Urban--suburban relationships
   g. Relationships between types of libraries
4. Education of Librarians
   a. How can they be prepared for decision-making?
   b. How are attitudes shaped by library education?
   c. How can they move from passive to active performance levels?
5. Library Operations
   a. How can two-way exchange between user and library be developed?
   b. Factors insuring accessibility and relevancy.
   c. Advantages and disadvantages of centralization and de-centralization.
   d. Optimum size of systems
   e. Optimum structure of systems
   f. Basis for computing reimbursement in systems, among libraries, between jurisdictions.

      g. Method of analyzing effectiveness of library public
          relations.
      h. Examination of constraints
          Governmental structure
          Civil Service
          Unions
      i. How does source of funds affect library priorities
          e.g., Federal priorities may become local priori-
          ties in order to receive funds.
    6. Library Services
      a. Evaluation of present services
      b. Analysis of unmet needs
      c. Formulation of alternative methods of meeting needs.

A few of these are currently being investigated: impact of federal funds, measurement of effectiveness of public libraries, service to the urban poor, users versus non-users. Priorities need to be established and the components of this research effort coordinated to insure implementation and funding of priority items and elimination of unnecessary duplication. A coordinator with research competence and an advisory panel will be required.

Third, continued coordination to insure wide dissemination of the results of the research, the development of prototypes and application in real life through demonstration.

Fourth, an intensive educational effort within the formal structure of library education and in informal continuing education is necessary. There are indications that some of this is happening already. AALS has focused on continuing education at its meeting at this Mid-winter Conference and adopted a plan of action. Library schools are recognizing the need through curriculum revision. State library agencies are attacking the problem. In fact, in some areas there may be danger of over-kill as continuing education dealing with certain problems is duplicated unnecessarily while other needs are neglected. A PLA task force on the continuing education of public librarians needs to establish liaison with AALS, LED, ASL and the Bureau of Libraries, to establish priorities, survey present offerings and seek funds with the assistance of the National Commission on Libraries. Among public librarians there is a critical need to know:

    1. How to determine the library and information needs of
       each community
    2. How to develop plans--set goals--with, nor for, users.
    3. How to communicate what the library is doing so that
       it become truly visible.
    4. How to manage libraries so effectively that they will
       receive needed support.
    5. How to perform actively, not passively.
    6. How to change and help others to change.

Steps Toward Implementation of These Recommendations

      Either the president of the Public Library Association and the PLA Board should assume direct responsibility, or a task force on A Strategy for Change in the Public Library, responsible to the president of PLA, should be established immediately and seek support, implementation within public libraries, in related divisions of ALA and in other components of the profession, the National Commission on Libraries, the Council on Library Resources, and the Bureau of Libraries in the Office of Education, the National Endowment for the Humanities and other governmental and non-governmental sources. A plan of action should be devised, sources of funds for implementation should be located, and implementation of the plans should have begun by the June, 1972 meeting of ALA in Chicago. Such a plan is not only essential for strong development of the public library, it will invigorate the Public Library Association.

Resources for Problem Solving, Planning and Development

The following resources already available to public libraries were identified:

Research in Progress

1. <u>The Measurement of Effectiveness of Public Libraries</u>--conducted by the Bureau of Library and Information Science Research, Graduate School of Library Service, Rutgers, under the direction of Dr. Kenneth E. Beasley, Dean of the Graduate School, University of Texas at El Paso, with ALA (PLA) sponsorship. The project is to develop and test new types of measuring devices for assessing public library services. Such devices will be closely related to questions such as: how well a library meets the needs of its community; its awareness of potential and unexpressed needs; and its capacity for long-range planning while maintaining flexibility.

This study promises to help answer the imponderable, "Can public library service be measured?" It will provide assistance to management seeking to base accountability on solid data. The project is moving on schedule with completion anticipated in 1972.

2. <u>The Indiana Library Studies</u>--One of the most extensive studies ever undertaken at the state level is this group of projects under the direction of Dr. Peter Hiatt. The summary volume, Number 20, will be completed early in 1972. Some of the studies are applicable only to Indiana but many are relevant anywhere and the approach has broad implications for library studies at any level.

The two studies which are most widely applicable are:

Volume I. <u>Response To Change: American Libraries in The Seventies</u>, by Virginia H. Mathews, Deputy Director, National Library Week Program, and Dan Lacy, Senior Vice-President, McGraw-Hill Book Company. The volume is an examination of the major social and educational changes taking place in the United States, and their implications to library development, and

Volume X. <u>Survey of User Service Policies In Indiana Libraries and Information Centers</u>, by Dr. Edwin E. Olson, Associate Professor, School of Library and Information Service, University of Maryland. This volume is a landmark study which describes current library service policies in Indiana, and presents information which can have impact on the process of making decisions about future library services.

3. <u>Dallas Public Library Independent Study Project</u>--A demonstration which will determine the effectiveness of the public library

in informal continuing education. "The project will give assistance
toward a planned course of study, to helping people if they so desire
to achieve a two-year college education through their independent
study, studying on their own time, at their own speed, in the library,
at home or elsewhere."[1]

     4. A Systems Analysis of the Library and Information
Science Statistical Data System--Directed by Dr. Morris Hamburg,
Wharton School of Finance and Commerce, University of Pennsylvania.
Dr. Hamburg and his associates were concerned with the development of
decision models and statistical information systems for large public
libraries and university libraries. The demonstration phase of the
project was not funded by the USOE. The first phase is scheduled for
completion in mid-1972. The major thrust of the initial work in the
Interim Report to USOE is directed toward the development of a framework for library management systems. It is hoped that this can be
published; also three additional monographs based on the doctoral
dissertations of Michael Bommer, Leonard Ramist and Ronald Whitfield
which deal with development of framework for allocation of funds in
university, large public and state libraries.

     5. Lipsman, Claire. Library Service to the Disadvantaged--
Manuscript scheduled for publication by ALA based on research undertaken by the Behavioral Science Corporation, Washington, D. C. for
USOE. This study examines the factors that appear to be basic to
effective library programs for the disadvantaged. Based on examination of programs in progress the investigator makes specific recommendations which, if adopted, would result in decided changes in the
service programs to disadvantaged areas and in library administration.

     6. Project Aurora--Elyria (Ohio) Public Library--This is
an example of an innovative experiment conducted in a single library
with implications for others. Using a caseload approach in target
areas of the community, paraprofessionals called on families door-to-
door to inform them of library services and fill their requests. The
project has been funded for a second year. The techniques should be
studied and constructive facets of the experiment applied elsewhere.

     7. Casey, Genevieve / Project Director--Case Studies of
Service to the Aged in 10 Exemplary Libraries. Summary in November,
1971 American Libraries. To be published by Institute of Gerontology,
Michigan University.

     8. Casey, Genevieve / Project Director. Public Library
Service to the Urban Disadvantaged; a year long experimental curriculum 1970-71--Report in summer of 1972.

     9. Systems Development Corp. Evaluation of LSCA Service
to Special Target Groups--A project developed for the Bureau of
Libraries--Office of Education. To be completed Sept., 1972.

     10. Lange, Clifford E. Public Library Director-Board
Member Relationships: A Study of Attitude, Perception and Communication Behavior--Dissertation scheduled for completion Spring, 1972.

Surveys, Plans, Statistical Analysis

LSCA funds have been widely used for surveys and plans at state, regional and local levels. Every state but one has had either a statewide survey or state plan, or surveys of individual regions, countries and cities. These vary greatly in quality and in their impact, but, taken all together they form a substantial background for continuing study and research.

In the past, needed statistics collected at the national level have been published too late to be of great value. The National Center for Educational Statistics is making a concentrated attempt to establish consistency in information collected and to obtain distribution of this information much more promptly than heretofore as described in <u>Planning for a Nationwide System of Library Statistics</u>, prepared under contracts with the National Center for Educational Statistics of the U. S. Office of Education and submitted in May, 1970; published by the U. S. Government Printing Office.

Standards

Standards prepared for various types of libraries by divisions of the American Library Association have been a basis for comparison and a performance standard for many library plans and surveys. The Public Library Association is currently beginning a revision of Standards for Public Library Systems, 1966. Comments and suggestions made during the Proposed Public Library Goals Study pointed to the lack of credibility attached to standards as they have been developed in the past. The hope was expressed that any subsequent standards would be based on solid research.

Conferences, Institutes, Seminars

Other important sources of information on pressing problems and emerging trends in public library service are the papers presented at annual conferences sponsored by library schools, such as the University of Chicago, the University of Illinois at Allerton Park, Drexel, and others occuring less regularly. Many of these fall short of greatest benefit because publication of conference proceedings are long delayed or never reported. Conferences of the library associations should be another major source of current information. Public library institutes funded with federal funds at the various library schools have been in the minority. In some instances, difficulty in getting attendance from public libraries has been reported.

Research Centers, Research Specialists

The number of library schools with research centers, individuals specializing in library research and of commercial research firms concentrating on library study, has grown steadily in recent years.

If all of these sources of information could be identified and proceedings, papers, findings could be collected consistently and promptly, an impressive body of background information to assist public libraries would be available. The difficulty of locating this information is formidable. Results of a substantial number of research projects are never published. Information available through ERIC/CLIS is invaluable but great numbers of people attempting to cope with public library problems never have access to this information. ERIC/CLIS has proposed a Guide To Technical Document Procurement which would have as its purpose--To provide access to that large area of technical documents which are indexed, announced or distributed by the federal information services, and about which information is largely confined to the personal knowledge of librarians who attempt to obtain these documents. Such a guide is badly needed.

Although the number and kinds of library research and resource information relating to public libraries is growing it is minor when compared to research devoted to academic libraries. The number of projects funded and grants and fellowships awarded by the Council on Library Resources to public libraries and public librarians is minimal when compared to the academic library group. It appears that few applications come from public libraries. Theses and dissertations at library schools are infrequently directed toward public library problems.

NOTES

1/ David L. Reich. The Dallas Public Library Independent Study Project, Dallas Public Library, 1971, manuscript.

Selected Bibliography

This bibliography covering the period 1965-71, was selected from an extensive literature search covering the period 1950-71. The search provided background for this Feasibility Study for the Public Library Goals Project. Items dealing with the aims and objectives of all types of libraries--analyses, studies and reports which interpret the many facets of public library development since the Public Library Inquiry and those with implications for the public library in the future-- were examined. The amount of substantive information located was en- couraging; the inaccessibility of many of the items a major frustra- tion.

The most pertinent material was found in the period of 1965 to date. Also, literature searches covering the period prior to 1965 had been conducted as a part of research commissioned by the National Commission on Libraries eliminating the need to focus on the period 1950-65. Four other bibliographies include numerous additional re- ferences to individual surveys, development plans and studies of library cooperation:

1. Finnan, Anne. The Public Library: A Bibliography. ERIC/ CLIS.

2. Library Surveys and Development Plans; An Annotated Bibliography. Bibliography Series, No. 3. ERIC/ED031609, 1969.

3. Rike, Galen E. Statewide Library Surveys and Development Plans; An Annotated Bibliography, 1956-67. Illinois.

4. Stenstrom, R. H. Cooperation Between Types of Libraries, 1940- 1968: An Annotated Bibliography. American Library Associa- tion, 1970.

Altheide, D. L.
  "Is the Public Library Obsolete? Suggestions for Change."
  Mountain Plains Library Quarterly, 15:19-25, Summer, 1970."
    The author argues that "society needs a dynamic entity where people can meet, challenge, argue, change their opinions, and begin working to change society." The library should be this "awareness center."

American Library Association. American Association of State Libraries.
Standards Revision Committee.
    Standards for Library Functions at the State Level. Adopted
by the membership at the annual meeting June 22, 1969. American
Library Association, 1970.

American Library Association. Library Administration Division.
    Standards for Library Services for the Blind and Visually
Handicapped. Adopted July 14, 1966. American Library
Association.

American Library Association. Public Library Association. Audio-
visual Committee.
    Guidelines for Audiovisual Materials and Services for Public
Libraries. American Library Association, 1970.

American Library Association. Public Library Association.
    Minimum Standards for Public Library Systems, 1966. Adopted
July 13, 1966. American Library Association, 1967.

Anderson, J.
    "Who speaks for the Concerns of Library Service?" American
Libraries, 1:1062-8, December, 1970.
    The future of the public library. Who will shape the future?
What must be done? Anderson has specific answers.

Banfield, Edward C.
    The Unheavenly City: The Nature and Future of our Urban Crisis.
Little, Brown and Company, 1968.

Batchelder, M. L.
    Public Library Trustees in the 1960's. American Library Trustee
Association, American Library Association, 1969.
    A comprehensive study of trusteeship: historical background,
roles and responsibilities now and in the future.

Bendix, Dorothy, ed.
    Library Service for the Undereducated. (Conference of Library
Service to the Undereducated) Drexel Press, 1966.
    Combines viewpoints of sociologist and librarian on needs of
the undereducated and calls for commitment from librarians in
understanding the varied groups in this category.

Benford, John.
    "The Philadelphia Project." Library Journal, 96:2041-7. June
15, 1971.
    Describes the first phase of a study of school and public
libraries and plans to establish a new community library and
learning center--a new entity.

60

Benge, Ronald C.
 Libraries and Cultural Change. Archon, 1970.
  Emphasizes the humanistic responsibilities of libraries.

Berelson, Bernard.
 The Library's Public. Columbia University Press, 1949.

Blakely, R. R.
 "Wit to Win: Can Libraries Break Out of Their Four Walls."
 Maryland Libraries, 33:3-14, Fall, 1966.
  Reaching everybody through television, information systems,
 microforms. Bridging cultural gaps with new services.

Blasingame, Ralph, Jr.
 Research on Library Services in Metropolitan Areas. Rutgers
 University, 1966. (Follows Conant's The Public Library and the
 City.)
  Outlines areas needing research: 1) information need and
 supply, 2) social and political factors, 3) education and train-
 ing, 4) library operations, 5) history studies.

Bonser, Charles F. and J. R. Wentworth.
 A Study of Adult Information Needs in Indiana. Indiana Library
 Studies, Report 3, 1970. ERIC ED044133.
  Conclusions indicate that the public library has little relevance to the information needs of the adult population. Recommends matching needs of target groups with specific services
 which can be supplied. The findings here are applicable anywhere.

Brown, E. F.
 Modern Branch Libraries and Libraries in Systems. Scarecrow,
 1970.
  Surveys the library as it is. Lists areas needing research,
 including relative effectiveness of large versus small branches.

Bundy, Mary Lee, ed.
 The Library's Public Revisited. (Student Confrontation Series,
 No. 1) School of Library and Information Services, University
 of Maryland, 1967.
  Deals with contemporary problems not treated extensively
 elsewhere, including references to labor and the radical right.
 One essay, "The Suburban Reality and Its Implications for the
 Public Library," states the need for communal facilities in
 affluent suburbs.

Bundy, Mary Lee.
 *Metropolitan Public Library Users; a Report of a Survey of Adult
 Library Use in the Maryland-Baltimore-Washington Metropolitan
 Area*. 1968.
  Defines patron characteristics, describes factors influencing

public library use, and explores public opinion of libraries.
Major need: expanding types of service to increase clientele.

Burness, Carl G.
Defining Library Objectives. Wayne State University, 1968.
Defining objectives as a basis for PPBS (Planning-
Programming-Budgeting System).

Cazayoux, Vivian.
Public Library Services and Their Use by Professional Staffs of
Welfare Agencies. 1967. ED 045 151 ERIC.
Explores library programs of publicizing and interpreting
to professional welfare agency staff the collections and ser-
vices which they might use.

Chicago. University of. Graduate Library School.
Library Networks: Promise and Performance. 33rd annual conference. July 29-31, 1968. Ed. by Leon Carnovsky. University of
Chicago Press, 1968.
Analysis of comparisons between traditional and full-fledged
networks places the promise and performance of libraries in their
ability to coordiante services into a total service structure.

Chicago. University of. Graduate Library School.
Persistent Issues In Librarianship. 25th annual conference,
August, 15-17, 1960. University of Chicago Press, 1960.
Urban problems, adult education, library education, exten-
sion to unserved, leadership, money, cooperation, technology
were the issues in 1960.

Chicago. University of. Graduate Library School.
Public Library in the Urban Setting. 32 annual conference,
July 30-August 2, 1967. Ed. by Leon Carnovsky. University of
Chicago Press, 1968.
Analyzes social, governmental and educational developments
in metropolitan areas and their implications for libraries in
organization, financing, and meeting new needs of adolescents,
disadvantaged and ethnic groups, and suburbia. Emphasis not on
the "death of the library" but on the importance and challenge
of the library in meeting society's needs.

Cole, Fred.
Untitled working paper on the proposed role of the public library in non-traditional education. Presented to the Commission
on Non-Traditional Studies, August, 1971.
Proposes active role for public library in the movement for
the university without walls. Specific recommendations for implementing action.

Conant, Ralph W., ed.
The Metropolitan Library. To be published. (Updates The Public Library and the City).
The basic tradition of collecting and disseminating cultural and educational materials should continue, while extending definitions of user needs in accordance with vast social and technological changes of the future.

Conant, Ralph W., ed.
The Public Library and the City. MIT Press, 1965.

Conant, Ralph W.
"Sociological and Institutional Changes in American Life; Their Implications for the Library." ALA Bulletin, 61:528-36, May, 1967.
The extension of library education curriculum into other disciplines is a key factor in meeting the demands on libraries created by social change.

Constantine, J. Robert.
The Role of Libraries in the Cultural History of Indiana. Indiana Library Studies, Report 2, 1970. ERIC, ED044132.
Has been diluted by lack of funds. Stresses need for adequate funds if libraries are to meet cultural challenges. Local implications. Good example of historical approach.

Cousins, Norman.
"View of the American Library." ALA Bulletin, 61:953, September, 1967.
Discussion of the library as more than a depository; as a generative force and connective center.

Crowley, Terence and Thomas Childers.
Information Service in Public Libraries: Two Studies. Scarecrow Press, 1971.
Describes unobtrusive methods of measuring and evaluating information services. Studies revealed that libraries were disseminating outdated and incorrect information and were not aware of it.

Crum, Mark L., Jr.
What Does the Public Library User Really Want: The Accuracy of Library Personnel, Library Educators, and Library Board Members in Perceiving the Library-related Wants of Public Library Patrons. Western Michigan University, 1970.
Implications of study: changes in public library services, personnel recruitment and library school curricula based upon surveys of the preferences of the public, might be more sound than if based upon the library establishment.

Curley, M. T.
　　Buckram Syndrome:　A Critical Essay on Paperbacks in Public
　　Libraries of the U. S.　American Library Association, 1968.
　　(Public Library Reporter No. 13)
　　　　Survey revealed large libraries use more paperbacks but, in
　　general, paperbacks are considered by most as ephemeral material
　　rather than being utilized to full advantage.

Doms, Keith.
　　"Needed:　A Fuller Knowledge of the User and Nonuser."　Wilson
　　Library Bulletin, 41:931-2, May, 1967.
　　　　Basing library services on realistic analyses of users, con-
　　sidering access in terms of goals, attitudes, methods and
　　materials, and defining roles of school and public libraries
　　are suggested as most vitally needed.

Donohue, Joseph C. and Peppi, Carole.
　　The Public Information Center Project.　Enoch Pratt Free Library,
　　1971.　46 p.
　　　　A short term experiment which has practical implications for
　　other libraries considering the new information center concept.
　　Contains an account of Britain's C.A.B.'s.

Eastlick, John T., ed.
　　Changing Environment of Libraries.　Papers delivered at the
　　1970-71 Collegian Series, Graduate School of Librarianship,
　　University of Denver.　American Library Association, 1971.
　　　　". . . What the library environment will be in the future."

Eisner, Joseph.
　　"Public Libraries:　On the Skids?"　Library Journal, 96: 3094-5,
　　October 1, 1971.
　　　　Analyses of expected trends in the financial situation of
　　public libraries indicate that library funding will not keep
　　pace with increasing costs of library service and may require
　　changes in programs and goals for the future.

Ellis, Richard A., Sarah K. Thomson and Janet Weiss.
　　NIL:　A Study of Unfilled Interlibrary Loan Request in the NYSILL
　　System.　A report prepared for the Division of Library Develop-
　　ment of the New York State Library. Washington, D. C.　Nelson
　　Associates, Inc., 1970.
　　　　Study of reasons for failure to supply materials through the
　　state's interlibrary loan system revealed failures due to pre-
　　mature cancellations, inappropriate routing and missearching.

Ennis, Philip H.
Adult Book Reading In the United States: A Preliminary Report.
National Opinion Research Center, Report No. 105. University
of Chicago, 1965.
Inconclusive. Demonstrates an approach which may be used
in more extensive, conclusive research.

Ennis, Philip H.
The Library Consumer. Unpublished paper.
Libraries must set priorities of objectives. "It is neither
possible nor desirable to spell out a national program or national standards. Each public library must determine its own
community needs and proper structure."

Evans, C. W.
Middle Class Attitudes and Public Library Use. Libraries
Unlimited. Research Studies in Library Science, No. 9, 1970.
To increase use, recommends more business and vocation-
related services, public awareness and a more accurate concept
of the library.

Finnan, Anne.
The Public Library: A Bibliography. ERIC/CLIS
General bibliography for the use of those undertaking critical articles, state-of-the-art surveys and to identigy information gaps, as a base for decisions on the role of the public
library. Items listed under broad categories.

Foust, James D. and Carl B. Tower.
General Economic and Demographic Background and Projections
for Indiana Library Services. Indiana Library Studies, Report
5, 1970. ERIC ED044134.   (and)

Foust, James D. and W. R. Hughes.
Regional Supply and Demand for Library Services. Indiana
Library Studies, Report 6, 1970. ERIC ED044135.
Economic and demographic background and projections organized by state planning districts. This information was inter-
preted in terms of projected library use and costs. The model
would be useful anywhere. Only public circulation is used as
the basis of future use and projected costs.

Franklin, Hardy.
"Reaching the Non-User." Wilson Library Bulletin 41:1943-946.
May, 1967.
Lists research needs of libraries attempting comprehensive
service to the disadvantaged.

Frantz, J. C.
    "Big City Libraries: Strategy and Tactics for Change."
    Library Journal 93:1968-70, May 15, 1968.
        Using Brooklyn as an example, suggests reaching non-users
    through creative approaches, decentralization, more responsive
    services.

Frantz, J. C.
    "Outreach or Oblivion?" Wilson Library Bulletin, 43:848-903,
    May, 1969.
        Attempts to assess the role and goals of public libraries
    through a series of articles on the ghetto, the aged, American
    Indians, children and adults.

Gaines, E. J.
    "Informational Switching Yard: The Concept of the Library."
    Library Journal, 95: 641-, February 15, 1970.
        Proposes expanding the library to the major information
    resource center for the community. Might charge fees. Library
    a vital part of the community.

Gaines, E. J.
    "Urban Library Dilemma." Library Journal 94:3966-70, November
    1, 1969.
        Concentrate on resource and information center for business.
    Reduce services for children.

Garrison, Guy.
    Studies in Public Library Government, Organization and Support.
    Illinois University, Library Research Center, 1969.
        Studies cover areas of public library funding, service in
    suburban communities, public support and use of libraries,
    relationship of administrative structure to levels of service
    and factors of library system membership.

Geller, Evelyn.
    "This Matter of Media." Library Journal 96:2047-53, June 15,
    1971.
        Perceptive appeal for a new level of library performance
    relating print and non-print.

Goldhor, Herbert
    Effect of Prime Display Location on Public Library Circulation
    of Selected Adult Titles. (Unpublished paper) November, 1971.
        Study supports the hypothesis that books placed in a prime
    location to facilitate browsing will circulate more than when
    left in the library general collection. An example of an in-
    vestigation that could be applied elsewhere.

66

Goldstein, Harold, ed.
Changing Environment for Library Services in the Metropolitan
Area. Allerton Park Institute No. 12. Champaign, Illinois,
1966.
     Useful in providing a total picture of the library in the
urban setting and for understanding the interrelationship between libraries and the metropolitan environment.

Gould, Samuel B.
"New Era for the Public Library." ALA Bulletin, 60:585-90, June,
1966.
     Suggests goals based on anticipated societal needs. This
paper, presented five years ago, is more relevant today than
when published.

Grabowski, Stanley M.
"ERIC Special Degree Programs for Adults." Adult Leadership,
pp. 75-76, June, 1971.
     An annotated bibliography.

Gregory, Ruth W. and Lester Stofel.
Public Libraries in Cooperative Systems: Administrative Patterns
for Services. American Library Association, 1971.
     "As a result of system membership, the local public library
will be equal to the challenge of the last quarter of the century."
A hard look at cooperative system operation.

Grimes, George.
Information Services: Survey of History and Present State Of
Field. Michigan-Ohio Regional Education Laboratory, 1969.
     Summarizes and relates educational information services and
laboratories: (1) information networks; (2) information transfer;
(3) specialized information centers; (4) mechanization, information science.

Hall, Anna C.
Selected Educational Objectives for Public Service Librarians:
A Taxonomic Approach. Thesis, University of Pittsburg, 1968.
     A scientific comparison of educational needs of public
librarians and the library school curriculum. Elements in the
needs were not met by the library school curriculum.

Hamburg, Morris.
A Systems Analysis of the Library and Information Science
Statistical Data System: The Preliminary Study. Interim Report.
ERIC ED035421.
     Only first phase funded.

Hannigan, M. C.
"Orientation of the Out-Of-School Adult to the Use of the Public

Libraries." <u>ALA Bulletin</u>, 61:829-30, July, 1967.
     Provides guidelines for "painlessly" orienting adults to
library use, which focus on eliminating fears and anxieties that
deter individuals from using the library.

Haro, R. P.
     "How Mexican Americans View Libraries; a One Man Survey."
     <u>Wilson Library Bulletin</u>, 44:736-42, March, 1970.

Havighurst, H. L.
     "Educational Changes: Their Implications for the Library."
     <u>ALA Bulletin</u>, 61:537-43, May, 1967.
     Need for humanistic approach to continuing education to
counteract technology.

Heal, E.
     "Bookmobiles: A Somewhat Closer Look." <u>American Libraries</u>,
     2:72-8, January, 1971.
     Recommends methods for upgrading bookmobile service.

Hess, Edward J.
     <u>A Study of Human Response to California Library Organization and
     Management Systems</u>. Dissertation. University of Southern
     California, 1970.
     Based on the assumption that library staff are a social
system and determine goals of libraries. All processes for
effective production were favorable except performance goals
and training.

Hiatt, Peter.
     "How Do You Change a Change Agent?" or "The Indiana Library
     Studies From Conception to Fulfillment." <u>Library Occurrent</u>,
     23:191-203, May, 1970.
     Hiatt traces the history of the studies and suggests acti-
vity to follow.

Hiatt, Peter and H. T. Drennan, eds.
     <u>Public Library Services for the Functionally Illiterate: A
     Survey of Practice</u>. Sponsored by the Committee on Services to
     the Functionally Illiterate. Public Library Association,
     American Library Association, 1967.
     Includes examples of activities and list of people involved
in program.

Hicks, Warren B. and A. Tillin.
     <u>Developing Multi-media Libraries</u>. Bowker, 1970.
     The concept of the modern library as a comprehensive re-
source center. Philosophy and objectives of the center are
clarified and desirable practices in the selection and acquisition

68

of non-book or A-V materials are recommended, along with information pertinent to facilitating these tasks. Organization--
cataloging and physical processing--flexible practices--examples
of work--flow charts--standardized procedures.

Hillard, J. M.
    "Profession Gone Mad; a Librarian Urges a Return to the Proposals
    in the Public Library Inquiry." Library Journal 95:42-3,
    January 1, 1970.
        Pleads for traditional print services. Contains reaction
    from Eli Oboler.

Houser, L. J.
    Indices of Effectiveness of Public Library Services: Relation-
    ship of Registrants and Financial Support. Thesis. Rutgers
    University, 1968.
        Public libraries continue to attract primarily middle and
    upper classes, thus questioning the validity of the "area served"
    concept on which much library service is based.

Hutcherson, Ethel M.
    "The Role of the Public Library in Retraining People Displaced
    by Technological Change." Florida Libraries, 18:17-18, 1967.
        Most library administrators felt responsibility supportive.
    Larger population centers also provided retrieving programs.

Illinois. University. Urbana. Graduate School of Library Science.
    Cooperation Between Types of Libraries: The Beginnings of a
    State Plan for Library Service in Illinois. Ed. by Cora
    Thomassen. Allerton Park Institute, No. 15. University of
    Illinois, 1969.
        Stresses opportunities for cooperation in processing centers,
    and in emerging industrial information services.

Illinois. University. Urbana. Graduate School of Library Science.
    Federal Legislation for Libraries. Ed. by Winifred Ladley.
    Allerton Park Institute No. 13. University of Illinois, 1967.
        Collection of articles by authorities in the field, studies
    of the impact of federal legislation on libraries--public,
    academic, government and special--and on library education.

Indiana Library Studies.
    No. 20. Unpublished. By Peter Hiatt.
    This is to be a synthesis of the nineteen studies.

Indiana. State University. Terre Haute.
    Changing Concept of Service in Libraries: A Centennial Lecture
    Series and Symposium. 1970.
        Interchange between students and practicing librarians

revealed that librarians must be innovators by changing services to meet the diverse social, economic and educational backgrounds of their communities.

Javelin, M. C.
"How Local Government Agencies and Public Libraries Pool Their Resources for the Individual's Continuing Education." ALA Adult Services Division Newsletter, 7:51-2, Summer, 1970.
Describes the establishment of two-way communication between a library and local agencies, and how they cooperated in devising programs for the disadvantaged.

Jenkins, Harold R.
"The ABC's of PPB; an Explanation of How Planning-Programming-Budgeting Can Be Used to Improve the Management of Libraries." Library Journal, 96:3089-93, October 1, 1971.
Discusses requirements for application of PPB to libraries. Suggests system has potential for promoting the most constructive utilization of resources and personnel.

Jennison, Peter S. and Robert N. Sheridan.
The Future of General Adult Books and Reading in America. American Library Association, 1970.
Trends in readership are reviewed by editors, critics, librarians, publishers, authors, and media specialists. Consensus: quality and quantity of adult reading will increase due to population growth, greater urbanization and better education.

Jordan, R. T.
Tomorrow's Library: Direct Access and Delivery. Bowker, 1970.
Summary of direct services: mail, phone, drive-up, delivery. Not enough experience to be conclusive.

Joy, Patricia L.
Young Adults Service in Connecticut Public Libraries. MLS. Southern Connecticut State College, 1968.
Findings in this study indicated that few libraries had separate young adult collections; high school students generally made greater use of reference collections than adults; most libraries had no real contact with the schools; and little compliance was found with ALA standards.

Kahn, Herman and Anthony I. Wiener.
The Year 2000: A Framework for Speculation on the Next Thirty-Three Years. Macmillan Company, 1967.

Knight, Douglas M.
    "Wisdom in Action: The Role of the Modern Library." Connecticut
    Libraries, 12:3-7, Summer, 1970.
        Stresses the role of the public library as mediator be-
    tween the public and persons of special knowledge, and urges
    cooperation among libraries and all community agencies.

Knight, Douglas M. and E. S. Nourse, eds.
    Libraries at Large. Bowker, 1969.
        Public libraries viewed by librarians and users in this
    resource work based on studies commissioned by the Commission
    on Libraries.

Kortendick, James J. and Stone, Elizabeth W.
    Job Dimensions and Educational Needs in Librarianship. A.L.A.,
    1971.
        Concentrates on post-masters educational needs but has im-
    plications for library education at any level. Identifies
    current educational needs based on job requirements.

Kronus, Carol Lefson.
    Inducing Attitudinal Change Among Librarians: An Evaluation of
    the Institute on Public Library Service to the Inner City. 1970.
        An experiment measuring the amount of attitudinal change
    resulting from participation in the institute revealed signifi-
    cant changes on: community involvement, urban poor and institutes
    as educational devices.

Lacy, Dan and V. H. Mathews.
    Social Change and the Library, 1945-80. Final Report to the
    National Advisory Commission on Libraries. 1967.
        Future responsibilities of libraries include: (1) supporting
    formal education; (2) sustaining complex operations of govern-
    ment and economy; (3) providing opportunities for continuing
    education; (4) playing a role in reintegration of disadvantaged
    into society and (5) providing resources for an informed public
    and for personal growth.

Lasswell, H. D.
    "Library as a Social Planetarium." American Libraries, 1:42-3,
    February, 1970.
        Society and all knowledge are on a continuum, with libraries
    at the center of the "galaxy," surrounded by schools, colleges,
    media, and other sources for meeting needs of the public.

Lee, Robert Ellis.
    Continuing Education for Adults Through the American Public
    Library, 1833-1964. American Library Association, 1966.

        This history of varying emphasis: enlightenment, personal

development, cooperation, access. Now community development
serves as a reminder and basis for planning adult education
services in the future.

Leigh, Robert D.
The Public Library in the United States: The General Report
of the Public Library Inquiry. Columbia University Press, 1950.

Leimkuhler, F. F. and A. E. Neville.
"Uncertain Future of the Library; with Comment by W. S. Dix, R.
D. Rogers, and R. G. Vosper." Wilson Library Bulletin, 43:30-43,
September, 1968.
    In the near future, libraries should hold everything on
everything. In the distant future, automation replaces the
book. Dissenting opinions included.

Lemke, A. B., ed.
Librarianship and Adult Education: A Symposium. Syracuse
University School of Library Science. 1963.
    The psychology of adult education--reappraisal of adult
education--and response to community needs.

Library Surveys and Development Plans; an Annotated Bibliography.
Bibliography Series, No. 3. ERIC ED031609. 1969.
    Lists 104 library surveys and development plans at the
state or national level published since 1965.

Lipsman, Claire.
Library Service to the Disadvantaged. 1971. Unpublished
manuscript.

Little, Arthur D., Inc.
The Role of the Public Library in Maine: Consumer Needs and
Attitudes Towards Public Librarians in Maine. (The author), 1970.
    Survey identified public attitudes on libraries, and how
they affected use.

Little, Arthur D., Inc.
The Urban Central Library: Development Alternatives for San
Francisco. (The author), 1970.
    This survey of the San Francisco Public Library uses the
market survey approach. Needs of the community are clearly
identified, goals sharply defined.

Luce, R. J.
"Model Cities Community Information Center, Philadelphia."
American Libraries, 1:206-7, February, 1971.
    One city's experience with an automated telephone informa-
tion center. System more sophisticated than required.

Lyman, Helen Huguenor, ed.
"Library Programs and Services to the Disadvantaged." Library Trends, Vol. 20, No. 2, October, 1971.
A substantial contribution to library literature pulling together reports of library service to many groups within the large segment called "disadvantaged." The single most significant factor in serving the disadvantaged persons and groups may be the respect and understanding between the user and library personnel. "It is imperative to know and appreciate the life styles, cultural beliefs and values, motivations, desires, interests and aspirations of various groups."

McClarren, Robert R.
Community Analysis. North Suburban Library System, 1971.
Essential steps: (1) planning; (2) collecting data, (3) organizing data; (4) interpretation of data; (5) re-evaluating program; (6) reporting; (7) continuing study.

MacDonald, B.
Literacy Activities in Public Libraries; a Report of a Study of Services to Adult Illiterates. American Library Association, 1966. ERIC ED010855.
Obstacles to serving illiterates: lack of knowledge, skills, and ideas by librarians, and lack of coordination with other agencies which deal with illiterates.

Maloney, Ruth May.
"Average Director of a Large Public Library." Library Journal, 96:443-5, February 1, 1971.
Results of a survey indicated: no significant change in the characteristics of directors since 1903, except they are now more qualified, and more often men. Concludes that libraries are status quo, and may stay that way.

Marchant, M. P.
The Effects of the Decision-Making Process and Related Organizational Factors on Alternative Measures of Performance in University Libraries. Doctoral Dissertation. University of Michigan, 1970.
Study of managerial-style effect on service in university libraries, but with implications for public libraries as well.

Markuson, Barbara Evans.
"An Overview of Library Systems and Automation." Datamation, 16: 60-8, February, 1970.
Unique characteristics of library operation which may be restrictive to the use of automation are outlined, and include interdependence of libraries, user needs and demands, and physical limitations.

Martin, Lowell A.
     Baltimore Reaches Out: Library Service to the Disadvantaged.
     Enoch Pratt Free Library, 1967.
          ". . . an inquiry into the reading potential of city resi-
     dents of limited cultural and educational background and the
     role which the public library can and should play in serving
     these people." (p. 126, Bundy. Metropolitan Library Users).

Martin, Lowell A.
     "Suburban Systems in Metropolitan Library Networks." North
     Suburban Library System (Morton Grove, Illinois) Proceedings,
     September 18, 1969. North Suburban Library System, 1970.
          Describes the uniqueness of a suburban library system, its
     roles in the metropolitan library network and the potential of
     suburban systems for experimentation.

Martin, Lowell A., and others.
     Library Response to Urban Change; a Study of the Chicago Public
     Library. American Library Association, 1969.
          A detailed plan for Chicago which has general implications.

Mathews, Virginia.
     Neighborhood Library Centers and Services; A Study of the National
     Book Committee for the Office of Economic Opportunity. National
     Book Committee, 1967.
          A blue print for the emerging pattern of services in low-
     income areas.

Mathews, Virginia and Dan Lacy.
     Response to Change: American Libraries in the Seventies. Indiana
     Library Studies, Report 1, 1970. ERIC ED044131.
          Effects on libraries nationally resulting from population
     shifts and growth and increased scientific research and develop-
     ment.

Melcher, Daniel and Margaret Saul.
     Melcher on Acquisitions. American Library Association, 1971.
          Calls for understanding of what is possible. Stresses
     planning, research, better management to insure patron quick
     service.

Mendelsohn, H. A. and K. Wingerd.
     Use of Libraries and Conditions That Promote Their Use; a Report
     to the National Advisory Commission on Libraries. Academy for
     Educational Development, Inc., 1967.
          Based on literature, Gallup Poll. Sustains Berelson study.
     Calls for intensive study of objectives.

74

Middlemiss, R. W.
"Books Are Only Half the Job." _Focus_, 23:169, December, 1969.
The other half is in providing incentive, options and discreet choice, making better use of forums, meetings and panels.

Minder, T. L.
"Organizational Problems in Library Cooperation." _Library Journal_, 95:3448-50, October 15, 1970.
Discuss human factors of cooperation. Need design data, training for research and development. Use tools of science, engineering and professions.

Minder, T. L.
The Regional Library Center in the Mid-1970's; a Concept Paper. Graduate School of Library and Information Science, 1968. University of Pittsburgh.
A projection of a concept and what it can accomplish; the Pittsburgh Regional Library Center.

Molz, K.
"Public Library: The People's University?" _American Scholar_, 34:95-102, Winter, 1964-65.
Why metropolitan libraries do not meet the needs of the urban poor.

Molz, K.
"State of the Art of Public Library Orientation; Keynote Address to the Preconference on Orientation, San Francisco, June 23, 1967." _Maryland Libraries_, 34:10-17, Winter, 1968.
Discusses importance of orientation, failure of librarians in this area, and what can be done for more effective orientation.

Molz, K.
"World Without Walls." _Arizona Librarian_, 27:9-21, Winter, 1971.
Explores dimensions in which mass media are changing the librarian's professional role.

Monat, W. R., and others.
Public Library and Its Community; a Study of the Impact of Library Services in Five Pennsylvania Cities. Pennsylvania State University, 1967.
Unawareness and general apathy on the part of the public as to library programs is greatly responsible for the public library's "identity crisis" and requires that librarians assume leadership in developing the full potential of the public library, and establishing its full identity.

Monroe, M. E.
"New Patterns for Library Service." _Library Journal_, 91:1366-70, March 15, 1966.

Designs for comprehensive services using all resources, all kinds of libraries.

Moon, E. E., and K. E. Nyren., eds.
Library Issues: The Sixties. Bowker, 1970.
This collection of Library Journal editorial essays grouped by topic summarizes the major concerns: federal aid (all types of libraries), intellectual freedom, discrimination, the library as a social agent, unions, and associations.

Moore, Everett T., ed.
"Intellectual Freedom." Library Trends, p. 168, July, 1970.
Where we stand on the matter of freedom to read and on access to libraries. The state of library freedoms and of our strengths and weaknesses in the war on ignorance and unreason.

Moreland, G. B.
"Operation Saturation: Using Paperbacks, Branch Libraries in Maryland Conduct an Experiment to Equate Book Supply With Patron Demand." Library Journal, 93:975-9, May 15, 1968.
This practical demonstration goes beyond recommending the use of paperback books. It refutes the "paperbacks instead of libraries" concept. Instead, it says, "paperbacks and libraries."

Morey, George Edward.
The Identification of Common Library Goals, Objectives, and Activities Relative to a Planning, Programming, Budgeting System. MLS Thesis, Western Michigan University 1970.
Study revealed that public library goals, while widely agreed upon, are not structured sufficiently to meet the PPBS requirements.

Morgan, M.
"Wrestling With the Angels; Emory University Institute on Public Library Programs for Youth." Mississippi Library News, 34:18-20, March, 1970. Orientation toward effective use of libraries.

Nelson Associates, Inc.
Public Libraries in the U. S.; Trends, Problems and Recommendations. Nelson Associates, 1967.
Focuses on both short-range and long-range concerns. Calls for a national commission to guide research and development and a national comprehensive plan for library service. Specific short-range recommendations deal with funds, metropolitan libraries, reference centers, Library of Congress, library standards, disadvantaged, advisory commission on state libraries.

Nelson Associates, Inc.
     Public Library Systems in the U. S.; A Survey of Multi-
     jurisdictional Systems. Nelson Associates, 1969.
          Examination of the operations of public library systems.
     Recommends additional study of management problems--measurement
     of effectiveness. No mention of the goals of libraries or their
     achievements.

New York. State Education Department.
     Report of the Commissioner of Education's Committee on Library
     Development. New York: State Education Department, 1970.

New York. State Education Department.
     Towards a Common Goal; School--Public Library Cooperation.
     Selected articles. New York State Education Department, 1968.
          A collection of articles covering general problems, opportu-
     nities, relationships and describing specific programs.

Nolting, O. F.
     Mobilizing Total Library Resources for Effective Service.
     American Library Association, 1969.
          An outsider summarizes the barriers to cooperation and the
     potential.

North, J. B., and others.
     Libraries and Industry; Background Study for Use by the National
     Advisory Commission on Libraries, 1967.
          Principle focus on industries serving libraries. Recommen-
     dations dealing with libraries serving industry and business con-
     cerned with interlibrary loan, copyright, funding, user study.

Nyren, E. K.
     "Notes on a Triangle: the Second Information Industry Associa-
     tion Annual Meeting in Washington, D. C., March 23-25, 1970."
     Library Journal, 95:1803-6, May 15, 1970.
          Concerned with responsibility and relationships of "for
     profit," "non-profit" and governmental agencies.

O'Brien, K. L.
     "Library and Continuing Education." Library Trends, July, 1968.
          Examines adult education services to a wide range of indivi-
     duals and groups. Found no consensus of the library's responsi-
     bility for adult education, active or passive.

Oko, D. K. and B. F. Downey.
     Library Services to Labor. Scarecrow, 1963.
          The needs of labor--what are they?

Olson, Edwin E.
Interlibrary Cooperation: Final Report. Maryland University.
School of Library and Information Service, 1970. ERIC ED046421.
Findings, based on study of sixty-eight systems throughout
the U. S., describe current roles, manpower needs, emerging pro-
totypes and readiness to change of interlibrary cooperation.
Part of a program to study manpower in library and information
professions.

Olson, Edwin E.
Survey of the User Service Policies in Indiana Libraries and
Information Centers. Indiana Library Studies, Report 10, 1970.
ERIC ED044139.
Detailed user study on libraries and information centers in
one state. Report provides methodology, findings based on
questionnaire, descriptive data, tables and weights obtained in
study.

Overmeyer, L.
Library Automation; a Critical Review. U. S. Office of Education,
Bureau of Research, 1969.
Gives account of use of automation in selected libraries
country-wide and discusses the fundamental considerations in
planning and implementation.

Owens, M.
"Model Library for Community Action." Library Journal, 95:1701-4,
May 1, 1970.
Detailed description of services essential for successful
ghetto library service.

Pepinsky, Harold B., ed.
People and Information. Pergamon Press, 1970.
Personal and societal implications of the information
revolution, human involvement in the production of information,
problems of information processing, and relationships between
information processing and political thought and action are
among the topics included.

Pfister, R. L. and J. W. Milliman.
Economic Aspects of Library Service in Indiana. Indiana Library Studies, Report 7, 1970. ERIC ED044136.
Experimental, exploratory attempt at benefit--cost analysis
of library services. Questions raised by economists. Comparisons of library objectives with actual use is still essentially the same as the Public Library Inquiry. Important
for its emphasis on the critical need for more data collecting
by libraries.

78

Prentice, Ann E.
The Public Library Trustee and Library Finance. Dissertation.
Columbia University, (in progress).
Aimed at determining the relationship between the public
library trustee's role perception and his effectiveness in
obtaining library funds.

Presthus, Robert
Technological Change and Occupational Response: A Study of
Librarians. Final report, Project No. 07-1084. Washington,
D. C., Office of Education, Bureau of Research, 1970.

Reich, David L.
The Dallas Public Library Independent Study Project. Dallas
Public Library, Texas, 1971.
An experiment funded by the National Endowment for the
Humanities in which the library assumes an active role in
adult non-traditional education.

Richer, Janet E.
Teacher Use of the Centerville Public Library Children's
Department. Thesis, Kent State University, 1968.
This study to assess the attitudes of elementary teachers
in a small midwestern city toward public library use, and
their actual practices in utilizing public library services
revealed that while many teachers applauded public library
use, very few practiced it.

Rike, Galen E.
State Library Surveys and Development Plans; An Annotated
Bibliography, 1956-67. Illinois State Library, 1968.
Lists, by state, all known surveys of libraries made during
the period and which were statewide in scope.

Robbins, Jane.
Public Library Policy Formation: Effects of Citizen Participation. Dissertation. University of Maryland, (in progress).
A study of citizen participation in the decision-making
processes in public libraries; to isolate and determine its
effect on library service.

Rohlf, R. H.
"Fear of Real Costs; Some Financial Aspects of the PLA Systems
Study." American Libraries, 1:242-4, March, 1970.
Explores advantages and disadvantages of different funding
methods in library systems and the barriers consolidation pose
to adequate and even service. Stresses need for budgetary
planning and concludes that library systems are generally poor
at managing their financial matters.

Rothines Associates.
>Centralized Processing for Indiana Libraries. Indiana Library
>Studies, Report 13, 1971.
>>Recommends an orderly, piece-by-piece approach to central-
>>ized processing for the state. Suggested steps in implementa-
>>tion might be adopted in other states with suitable variations.

Ruby, Carmela.
>Public Library Program for the Institutionalized. New Mexico
>State Library (study in progress).
>>An outreach project to re-integrate institutionalized persons
>>into the community, by introducing and orientating them to
>>library services.

Rutgers. University. Bureau of Library and Information Science
Research.
>Measurement of Effectiveness of Public Library Services. Ernest
>R. DeProspo, coord. American Library Association (in progress).
>>This project is seeking means of measuring public library
>>performance; the satisfier and dissatisfiers affecting use.
>>Scheduled for completion in 1972.

Sable, Arnold.
>"Whither Public Library Service in America." Wilson Library
>Bulletin, 45:390-3, December, 1970.
>>Compares the public library with railroads and the post
>>office and prophesies their demise. Suggests the public li-
>>brary will revert to earlier private status.

Schuman, P.
>"Two-day Maryland Meet Weighs Urban Libraries." Library
>Journal, 95:438-, February 1, 1970.
>>Reports the discussion between librarians and representa-
>>tives of other disciplines on informational, educational and
>>social responsibilities of urban libraries.

Shaffer, Kenneth R.
>"Library Systems: Tough Times Ahead?" Library Journal, 96:
>2263-5, July, 1971.
>>The main objective of library systems in the '60's (in-
>>creasing accessibility of materials) must now give way to that
>>of establishing a strong organization to withstand attacks of
>>censors, to make known the role of the library to the public
>>and to provide expertise in library operations for all sizes
>>and types of libraries.

80

Shaffer, Kenneth R.
"Suburban Library in the Affluent Ghetto (with discussion)."
(In North Suburban Library System, Morton Grove, Illinois,
Proceedings, November 21, 1968). North Suburban Library
System, 1969.

Shaughnessy, T. W.
Influence of Distance and Travel Time on Central Library Use.
Thesis, Rutgers University, 1970.
Study failed to detect any obvious differences in the
nature of central library use when examined in the context of
distance traveled.

Shaw, R. R.
"Quo Vadis; an Examination of the Librarian's Role in a
Democratic Culture." Library Journal, 92:2881-4, September 1,
1967.
Calls for active role. Success is measured by expanding
services, use, support.

Shera, J. H.
"What is Past is Prologue: Beyond 1984." ALA Bulletin, 61:
35-47, January, 1967.
A critique of library education. Cannot remain isolated.
Must be familiar with all disciplines while developing special-
ization. Call on expertise in non-library areas.

Shuman, Bruce A.
Empirical Determination of a Formula For the State's Contribution to Public Library Financing. Dissertation, Rutgers
University (in progress).
Research to develop a formula for accurately determining
the share of financial support to be provided by state govern-
ments for public libraries.

Simpson, D. J.
"Books and the Open University." Library Association Record.
September, 1971.

Sinclair, Dorothy.
Administration of the Small Public Library. American Library
Association, 1965.
A practical treatise. Stresses educational functions of
libraries, importance of systems.

Skellenger, James B.
Public Library Services in Portage County; an Analysis for Planning. Center for Urban Regionalism, Kent State University, 1970.
Plans for change in this library's services are formulated, based on analysis of library facilities and the population they serve, and patron opinions of needs.

Smith, Eleanor T.
"Libraries and Librarians in Our Changing Society." Minnesota Libraries, p. 339-47.
Has specific recommendations for objectives: be relevant, be an industrial agency, be the community information center, be cooperative.

Smith, Eleanor T.
"Reader Guidance: Are We Sitting Down On the Job?" Illinois Libraries, 48:527-32, September, 1966.
Describes methods of improving reader's services, stressing the importance of establishing relationships with patrons on an individual basis to better understand their needs.

Smith, Hannis S.
"A Seamless Web; the Systems Approach To Library Service." ALA Bulletin, 61:180-5, February, 1967.
A "seamless web" of library networks covering the U. S. and Canada, involving cooperative efforts of all types of libraries is proposed, established by law, with sound tax support and administrative structure.

Smith, L. P., ed.
Resources and Procedures for Improving the Indian American Use of Libraries. 1970.
Focuses on the relationship between the librarian and others involved in the learning situation for Indian youths, and on the needs for culturally relevant materials and extended services.

Stenstrom, R. H.
Cooperation Between Types of Libraries, 1940-1968: An Annotated Bibliography. American Library Association, 1970.
Indicates most cooperation still in talking stages with few results reported in 1968.

Stevenson, G. T., ed.
"Group Service in Public Libraries." Library Trends, Vol. 17, July, 1968.
Articles focus on reaching "the individual where he lives." Outlines needs and objectives of group services, and explores efforts of libraries in this area.

Stibitz, M. T.
"Adult Services in New York State; Community Involvement."
Bookmark, 28:48-52, November, 1968.
Describes community-oriented adult services in twelve New
York library systems.

Stoffel, L. L.
"Large City Library From the Viewpoint of the Suburban Library."
Library Quarterly, 38:90-100, January, 1968.
Large city libraries not assuming desired leadership in
developing cooperative services with suburbs.

Stone, C. W.
"A-V Task Force Survey Report." American Libraries, 1:40-4,
January, 1970. Comment: James Brown. "A Personal Viewpoint."
American Libraries, p. 44.
Major needs include improved A-V personnel training;
reliable information for librarians on A-V materials; and clear
definitions of strengthening A-V services. Comment by James
Brown suggests librarians must not only provide access to data,
but also be able to assist clientele in utilizing it to
meet needs.

Stone, C. W., ed.
"Library Uses of the New Media of Communication." Library
Trends, v. 16, October, 1967.
Covers wide range of media forms as they should or do
relate to libraries and reveals consensus of authors that
libraries are not adequately using new media. Calls for
redefinition of service concepts, new personnel training
methods, additional research and incorporation of other disciplines in library education in this area.

Stone, Elizabeth W.
"Continuing Education in Librarianship; Ideas for Action."
American Libraries, 1:543-51, June, 1970.
Nationwide access to continuing educational opportunities
is needed--a program which provides convenience, availability,
continuity and a wide range of choice.

Stone, Elizabeth W., ed.
"Personnel Development and Continuing Education in Libraries."
Library Trends, vol. 20, July, 1971.
Analysis of the techniques for developing the full potential
of library personnel, through planning, motivation, partici-
pation, training, evaluation and continuing library education.

Toffler, Alvin.
     "Anticipating Democracy." in <u>Future Shock</u>. Random, 1970.
     pp. 416-30.
         Calls for democratization of goal setting.

Voos, H.
     <u>Information Needs in Urban Areas: A Summary of Research in
     Methodology</u>, Rutgers, 1969.
         Part I of a research project under an OE grant, inquiring
     into "new bases" for library and information services in urban
     areas. Present techniques of measuring information needs are
     analyzed and evaluated in an attempt to determine their
     effectiveness as measures of urban population needs. Ex-
     tensive bibliography.

Wade, B.
     "How to Reach the Literate Adult Non-Readers." <u>Michigan
     Librarian</u>, 36:8-9, Summer, 1970.
         Suggests following services for the non-reader: record
     collections, exhibits, films, paperbacks.

Wasserman, Paul.
     <u>Toward a Methodology for the Formulation of Objectives in Public
     Libraries; an Empirical Analysis</u>. Doctoral dissertation,
     University of Michigan, 1960.
         An attempt to identify attitudes toward goal formulating
     in public libraries. Revealed the vagueness and haphazard
     formulation of presently existing objectives and greatly
     emphasizes the necessity of clearly defined, universal goals
     for the public library.

Winnberg, Alice M.
     <u>A Survey of the Literature Concerning the Work of the Public
     Library With the Community Hospital</u>. Catholic University of
     America Libraries, Washington, D. C., 1964.
         This history of the development of hospital librarianship
     and libraries explores problems that have been and are being
     encountered in meeting the standards of services to individuals
     in institutions.

Winsor, C. B.
     <u>Study of Four Library Programs for Disadvantaged Persons;
     Conducted By Bank Street College of Education</u>. Albany, New
     York, State Education Department, Division of Library
     Development, 1968. 3 vols. ERIC ED021592.
         A report of special library programs for the culturally
     disadvantaged in select New York areas which describes effects
     of projects on community and staff, recommendations for im-
     provements, and use of auxiliary personnel selected especially
     for the program.

Yocum, James.
    <u>The Development of Franklin County Public Libraries (Ohio), 1980</u>.
ERIC ED044160.
    Recommends: perfection of branch system; cooperation with
school libraries based on explicit contracts; centralized
reference collection and increased efforts to reach the non-
user.
    Seventy percent of the non-users studied said they would
not use the public library no matter what services were provided.